STO

CHARTERED FOR PROGRESS • TWO CENTURIES OF

AMERICAN BANKING

ELVIRA and VLADIMIR CLAIN-STEFANELLI, Curators, SMITHSONIAN INSTITUTION

A PICTORIAL ESSAY

REFERENCE

People liked to reproduce images of the Bank of the United States and its branches, even on china. A Staffordshire china vegetable dish with a view of the Savannah branch bank.

State Bank of New Brunswick

Will pay ONE DOLLAR to bearer on demand. NEW BRUNSWICK,

No. 6778 A

STATE OF ... NEW JERSEY

PENNSYLVANIA

THE MONONGAHELA VALLEY BANK

Will pay to bearer on demand. B

Five Dollars

McKEE'S PORT

No.

FIVE

Cashier

President

American Bank Note Company

5 5

REAL ESTATE PLEDGED.

EXCHANGE OFFICE

On demand after date We promise to pay the bearer FIVE DOLLARS

FIVE

Holly Springs Missi.

V V

Cash.

THE
State Bank
OF MICHIGAN.
LYMAN'S PROTECTION.

Bank Note on the right end mentioning
$1 One Dollar one third the length of the paper
$2 Two Dollars one half
$3 Three Dollars two thirds
$5 Five Dollars three fourths

American Bank Note Company, New York

DETROIT,   18
On demand
TWO DOLLARS
will be paid to bearer by the
STATE BANK of
MICHIGAN
TWO
Register
CASHIER
PRESIDENT
SECURED BY PLEDGE OF PUBLIC STOCKS

TWO   STATE OF   NEW-JERSEY.   TWO

2   2

TWO

The
STATE BANK of NEW-BRUNSWICK
Promises to pay Two Dollars on demand
to the bearer   New Brunswick   186

Cash.   Pres.

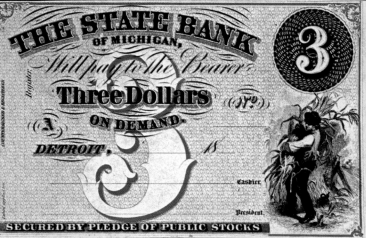

Lyman's Protection
Bank Note on the right end One Dollar covers one
third of the paper Two Dollars one half Three Dollars
two thirds Five Dollars three fourths.

American Bank Note Company

THE STATE BANK
OF MICHIGAN,
Will pay to the Bearer
Three Dollars
ON DEMAND.
DETROIT,   18
Register
3
Cashier
President
SECURED BY PLEDGE OF PUBLIC STOCKS

CHARTERED FOR PROGRESS • TWO CENTURIES OF

AMERICAN BANKING

A PICTORIAL ESSAY

TWO CENTURIES OF

CHARTERED FOR PROGRESS AMERICAN

BANKING

A PICTORIAL ESSAY

By **ELVIRA** *and* **VLADIMIR CLAIN-STEFANELLI,**

Curators, Smithsonian Institution

Published by **ACROPOLIS BOOKS, Ltd.**
Washington, D. C. 20009

Design & Cover	Henry J. Bausili
Consultants	Prof. Charles F. Haywood, Lexington, Ky.; Prof. Rondo Cameron, Atlanta, Ga.; The Honorable John W. Snyder, Washington, D. C.
Editing	Dr. Robert C. Post, Smithsonian Institution
Photography	David D. Blume; Alfred F. Harrell; Richard K. Hofmeister; Daniel Thompson; Sterling Jones, Smithsonian Institution
Color Photography	Adams Studio, Inc., Washington, D. C. and Erol Akyavas Photography

ACROPOLIS BOOKS LTD.
Colortone Building, 2400 17th Street, N.W
Washington, D. C. 20009

Printed in the United States of America
by COLORTONE PRESS *Creative Graphics, Inc.*
Washington, D. C. 20009

Library of Congress Cataloging in Publication Data
Clain-Stefanelli, Elvira Eliza.
Chartered for progress.

1. Banks and banking—United States—History—
Pictorial works. I. Clain-Stefanelli, Vladimir, joint
author. II. Title. III. Title: American banking.
HG2461.C57   332.1'0973   75-24641
ISBN 0-87491-032-3
ISBN 0-87491-031-5 pbk.

Table of Contents

Foreword

Banking arose in America coincidentally with the establishment of the nation; the first formal bank was founded during the War for Independence. From that time to the present, banking has been an integral part of our social history. In several periods, questions relating to banking have become the most pressing issues of their day; the special importance of banking has been dramatized during periods of great national need: wars, financial crises, and geographical and industrial expansion. The first banks reached directly only a small circle of people but over the years banks have increasingly been knitted into the fabric of society. Today, many millions of Americans have a personal and intimate relationship to the banking community.

The National Museum of History and Technology is first of all a museum of social history. Consequently, the exhibit *American Banking* falls in the middle of its area of concern. However, this is an unusual museum exhibit because the primary medium of the museum is the world of three dimensional objects. Banking and credit are in their essence services rather than "things." All the more remarkable, therefore, is the achievement of this exhibit which expresses the history of banking through a striking collection of objects, flat and three dimensional. It is these visual images which carry the present pictorial essay.

The early colonies had no banks, but, even more constricting, they had very little money of any sort. Barter was usual and, indeed, such commodities as tobacco formed the basis of exchange in some of the colonies. The characteristics of the colonial era —from the reliance upon tobacco receipts, through land banks, to bills of exchange—are expressed in this book more directly than they can be felt through words alone.

Banks answered an immediate need for money and credit, which, initially, they satisfied only in part. Yet, the vast needs of the expanding and growing nation called for ever more money and credit and for a great variety of services. Banks responded through inventiveness, trauma, conflict, and resolution—processes everywhere characteristic of American economic and political history. More and more, they succeeded in drawing abreast of enormously expanding national needs.

The book demonstrates the central importance of money; paper money, checks, and finally credit cards and electronic banking represent a central thread in the history of banking. Bank notes indeed are fundamental documents which chronicle both the development of banking and its expanding role in society. These are among the most important artifacts which express the essential function of banking.

Related objects, displayed in this book, document banking services. The graceful balance scale is not shown here as a craftsman's achievement but as evidence of the remarkable era of gold dust banking. The massive vault door is one evidence of the continuing need to provide security. Increasingly in the recent era, the technology of banking, from early check signing machines to the most sophisticated electronic equipment, represent artifacts through which the functions of banking can be seen.

Behind the money and behind the equipment associated with banks is the story of their intimate participation in the American experience. Perhaps the two most famous episodes when banking intersected American political history were the conflicts surrounding Andrew Jackson's veto of the renewal of the charter for the Second Bank of the United States and Franklin D. Roosevelt's reactions to the banking crisis of 1933. These dramatic episodes are presented here pictorially. Behind them, and also presented, is the quieter story of failure to establish a continuing central bank and final success in attaining a national banking system with the Federal Reserve System and a series of later institutions.

This Museum owes a debt of gratitude to many individuals and to many organizations for this exhibit—especially to the American Bankers Association for its generous financial assistance and to Joseph Wetzel Associates for its imaginative design. Deborah Bretzfelder of our Office of Exhibits served as project coordinator. Many staff members had a hand in *American Banking,* including Robert B. Korver, museum specialist; overall credit belongs to our two curators of numismatics, Vladimir and Elvira Clain-Stefanelli, who have invested enormous effort in carrying to successful completion this important exhibit. This book, based upon the exhibit, is the work of Elvira Clain-Stefanelli and of Vladimir Clain-Stefanelli.

Brooke Hindle
Director, The National Museum of
History and Technology
Smithsonian Institution

July 8, 1975

Colonial Banking Ventures

Barter Was Their Way of Life

1 / *Bartering for furs with the Indians.*

◄

"The great decay of trade, obstructions to manufactures and commerce in this Country, and [the] multiplicity of debts and suits thereupon [was] principally occasioned by the present scarcity of coin." These words depicted the sad financial situation predominant throughout the American colonies in 1686. The coins the early settlers had brought over were soon spent in setting up their homes, while new coin could not be freely obtained in the colonies because of rigid English regulations aimed at keeping specie ("hard cash") from leaving the mother-country.

This lack of coin forced the colonists to resort to exchange in goods—barter—or, as the people in Connecticut called it, "country pay." Barter had been their way of trading with the Indians, ex-

changing trinkets, gunpowder, and household objects for pelts of beaver, racoon, or fox. Necessity forced the colonists to trade the products of their soil with their white neighbors as well, and to pay their local taxes in corn, wheat, barley, rice, or other crop. The transporting of these bulky goods over primitive country roads and

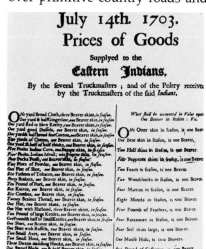

2 / *"One Shirt with Ruffles, two Beaver skins, in season . . ."* on a broadside of 1703.

3 / *Tobacco was shipped to England.*

the settling of accounts in perishable goods entailed losses and hardships which can hardly be comprehended today.

When the colonists sought better goods for their homes, or manufactured clothings, they had to import such "luxuries" from England. This kept the colonies chronically short of specie, since any that came in—from the West Indies mostly—soon found its way to England in exchange for imports.

The colonists had to supplement their payments for goods from England with lumber, pelts, rice, and especially tobacco. The saying that "tobacco was meat, drink, clothing and money" was indeed true, especially for Virginia and Maryland. Upon delivering their harvest to warehouses, planters would be handed a receipt or "crop note" representing a certain value. For almost two hundred years these were accepted in lieu of money for most payments including salaries and taxes. Virginia legalized tobacco warehouse receipts as currency in 1727. After shipment to England tobacco passed through the London Custom House where planters' agents would credit its value against expenses incurred for imports of English goods.

4 / *A receipt for 561 pounds of tobacco which probably changed hands quite often, being used as money in Virginia.*

5 / *John Winthrop, the Younger (1606-76), first Governor of Connecticut, one among the earliest supporters of banks.*

What was true of tobacco was also true of rice, especially in South Carolina, where "rice-orders," issued against anticipated yields, circulated as money, and beginning in 1719 were accepted even for taxes.

Interest in Banks

As life in the Colonies got more complex toward the end of the 17th century, the colonists began to feel hard-pressed for additional means of exchange to keep pace with the expanding economy. Many novel ways to facilitate credit were being debated in England, and the institution of a bank seemed a desirable solution. The year 1694 marked the founding of the *Bank of England,* an institution which proved its stability during many crises in the years to come. Almost half a century before, however, a book was published in London, entitled *A Key to Wealth or a New Way for Improving of Trade.* The author, William Potter, proposed an issue of paper money secured by holdings of land, the only form of wealth which could compete with gold and silver.

It was only natural that Potter's ideas found an echo in the New World where land was abundant, while gold and silver were scarce. In the 1660s John Winthrop, the Younger (1606-76), the Governor of Connecticut, proposed a similar land bank in his correspondence with members of the Royal Society of London. He regarded such a bank as "a foundation . . . for the advance of trade." Nevertheless, in 1686, when an attempt was made to found a land bank based on a proposal by Captain John Blackwell of Boston, the Massachusetts General Court refused to permit this private initiative.

Just four years later, however, on December 10, 1690, the colonial treasury of Massachusetts be-

15

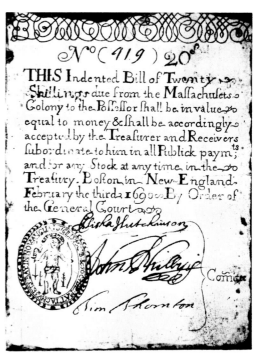

6 / *One of the first paper notes in the New World, issued in 1690 by the government of the Massachusetts Bay Colony.*

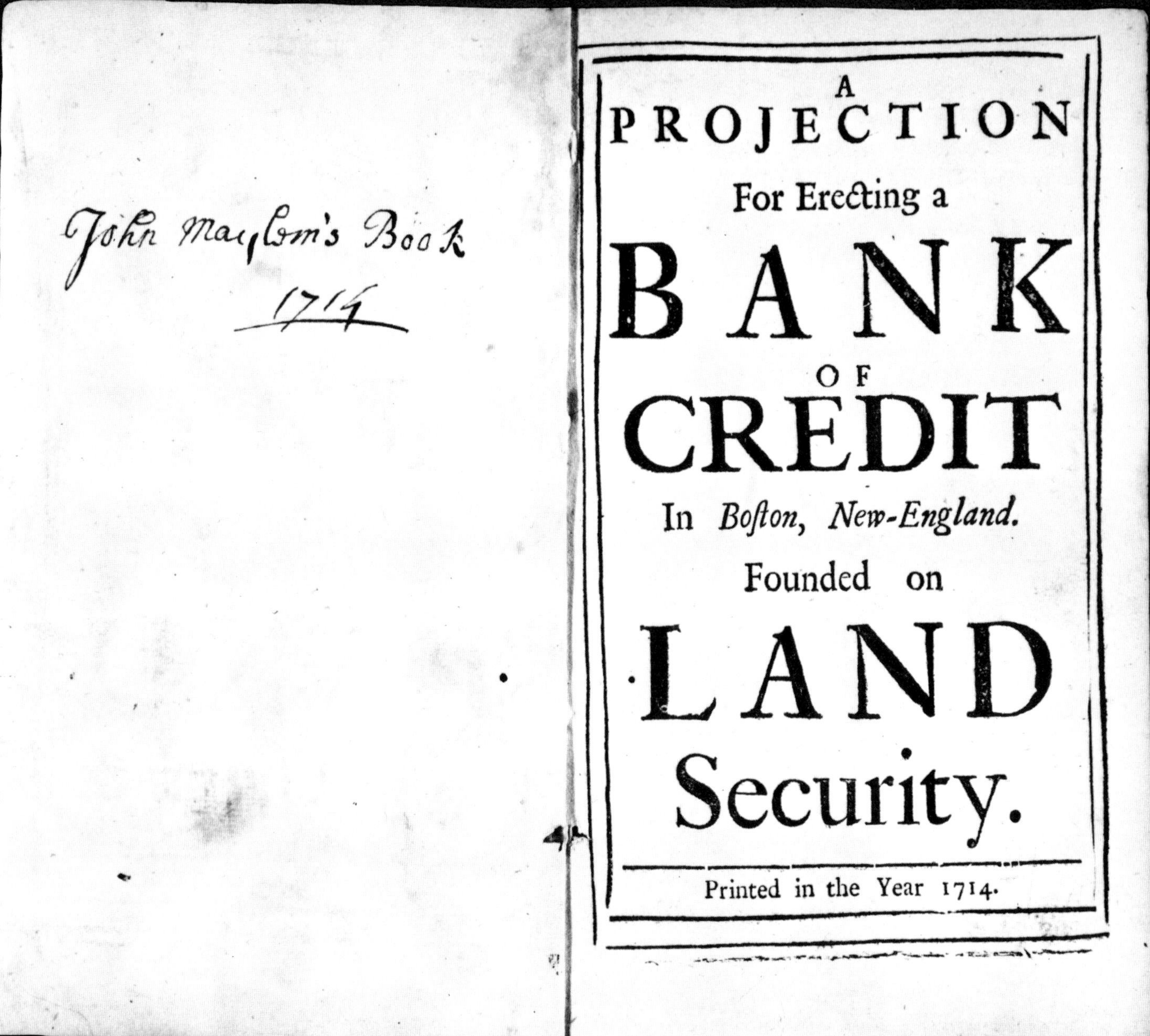

John Maylem's Book
1714

A
PROJECTION
For Erecting a
BANK
OF
CREDIT
In *Boston, New-England*.
Founded on
LAND
Security.

Printed in the Year 1714.

7 / "There being no other Expedient for the Reviving and Encouraging of Trade . . . but by Establishing a Fund or Bank of Credit upon Land Security. . . ."

8-10 / *John Colman, merchant of Boston, one of the first bankers in America; and one of his pamphlets written in support of his plans for a bank; a six shilling note, issued by Colman's land bank in 1740.*

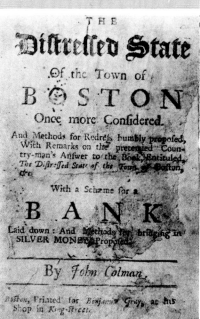

gan issuing its own paper notes in denominations of five shillings to five pounds. Intended to cover the expenses of a military expedition in French Canada, these notes constituted the first paper currency issued in the New World. They initiated a long series of similar issues by the governments of various colonies.

But such issues did not satisfy the needs of tradesmen. In 1714 a group met at the Sun Tavern in Boston whose concern was "the difficulties which the trade of this Province labors under, by reason of the scarcity of money." As a solution, these tradesmen proposed "a scheme of a bank of credit founded upon a land security," which was "to be undertaken and managed by persons of good

11 | Colman's idea of a land bank spread to other towns in New England and in May 1741 bank bills were privately issued in Ipswich, Essex County.

12 | A seven shilling sixpence note issued by the rival "Silver Bank" in Boston, 1740.

18

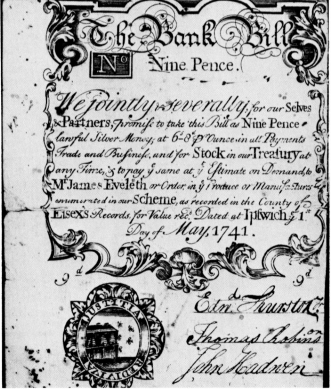

reputation, prudence and estates, in a voluntary partnership." In the end, however, the colonial legislature refused to charter this land bank.

Another group, the *New London Society United for Trade and Commerce,* received the same negative answer from the State of Connecticut when it petitioned for a bank charter in 1732. However, official rebuffs did not discourage these groups, which went ahead without charters and issued paper notes.

The First Bank of the Nation, The Land Bank

Among those who met at the Sun Tavern was an outstanding personality, John Colman, a promi-

13 / "Reported that the Bills proposed to be emitted by John Colman, Esq. and others would tend to endamage the Properties of His Majesty's good Subjects of this Province. . . ." With this justification Governor Belcher of Massachusetts prohibited the notes.

By His EXCELLENCY

JONATHAN BELCHER, Esq;

Captain General and Governour in Chief, in and over His Majesty's Province of the Massachusetts Bay in New England.

A PROCLAMATION.

WHEREAS a Scheme for emitting Bills or Notes by John Colman, Esq; and others, was laid before the Great and General Court or Assembly of this His Majesty's Province, in their Session held at Boston, the Fifth Day of December 1739, and by the Report of a Committee appointed by said Court was represented, if carried on, to have a great Tendency to endamage His Majesty's good subjects as to their Properties;

And whereas Application has been very lately made to Me and His Majesty's Council by a great Number of Men of the most considerable Estates and Business, praying that some proper Method may be taken to prevent the Inhabitants of this Province being imposed upon by the said Scheme; and it being very apparent that these Bills or Notes promise nothing of any determinate Value, and cannot have any general certain or established Credit;

Wherefore,

I Have thought fit, by and with the Advice of His Majesty's Council, to issue this Proclamation, hereby giving Notice and Warning to all His Majesty's good Subjects of the Danger they are in, and cautioning them against receiving or passing the said Notes, as tending to defraud Men of their Substance, and to disturb the Peace and good Order of the People, and to give great Interruption, and bring much Confusion into their Trade and Business.

Given at the Council Chamber in Boston, the Seventeenth Day of July 1740. In the Fourteenth Year of the Reign of Our Sovereign Lord GEORGE the Second by the Grace of GOD of Great Britain, France and Ireland, KING Defender of the Faith, &c.

J. BELCHER.

By Order of His Excellency the Governour, with the Advice of the Council,
J. Williard, Secr.

GOD save the KING.

WHereas the Committee of the Great and General Court or Assembly at their Sessions begun and held at Boston Dec. 5th 1739. Reported that the Bills proposed to be emitted by John Colman, Esq; and others would tend to endamage the Properties of His Majesty's good Subjects of this Province; and whereas a large Number of the principal Men of Estates and Business have petitioned His Excellency the Governour and Council to take such Measures as they in their Wisdom should think proper to prevent People's being imposed upon by the said Scheme commonly called the Land Scheme or Bank; whereupon the Governour & Council have issued a Proclamation warning and cautioning People against the said Bills: And we the Subscribers being abundantly perswaded that the said

Scheme, if carried on, will be of pernicious Consequence; and being willing and desirous to do what in us lies to prevent the said Imposition, hereby Agree, Declare and Promise, That we will not directly or indirectly by our selves or any for us, receive or take any Bills emitted on the said Scheme, commonly called the Land Bank: And we hereby caution and advise all Persons whatsoever who are indebted to us, or deal with us, that they refuse the said Bills and do not take any of them in Expectation of our receiving them at their Hands, we being determined not to take the said Bills for any Debts due, nor for any Goods, or on any Consideration whatever.

John Osborne	Thomas Green	Habijah Savage
Edward Hutchinson	John Spooner	Jonathan Armitage
John Alford	Joseph Dowse	James Allen
Samuel Welles	Robert Temple	William Bolean
Benjamin Lynde	Joseph Brandon	Nathaniel Vial
Joshua Winslow	Rufus Green	John Winslow
James Bowdoin	Samuel Demming	John Gibbins
Peter Fanueil	Thomas Palmer	John Tyler
James Smith	Stephen Bouteneau	Nathaniel Balston
Charles Apthorp	John Green	William Douglas
John Erving	Benjamin Green	Thomas Austin
Hugh Hall	Byfield Lyde	William Wyer
John Jekyl	Nath Showers	Andrew Hall
Benjamin Fanueil	Benjamin Hallowell	Benjamin Poilard
James Bouteneau	Peter Kenwood	John Trail
John Gooch	Thomas Childs	John Hill
Henry Caswell	Thomas Perkins	Joseph Fitch
Edward Tyng	Charles Paxton	Francis Johonnet
Nath. Cunningham	Samuel Wentworth	Thomas Lambert
William Silcomon	Robert Lightfoot	Joseph Gooch
William Lambert	James Gould	David Le Galley
Andrew Oliver	Ralph Inman	Jeremiah Green
Thomas Oxnard	John Hemmans	Isaac Gridley
Samuel Sewall	Thomas Lechmere	Benjamin Bagnall
Thomas Gunter	William Winslow	William Lance
Edmund Quincy	Joseph Lee	Josh Henshaw, jun
Josiah Quincy	Benjamin Bourn	David Wyar
Joseph Gerrish	Jacob Griggs	James Russell
John Barrel	Richard Clark	Andrew Newell
William Bowdoin	Henry Laughton	Robert Lewis
Francis Boreland	John Cutler	John Minot
John Fayerweather	John Dennie	Samuel Cary
Thomas Hutchinson	John Simpson	John Austin
Thomas Hubbard	Jonathan Simpson	Richard Sutton
Thomas Hancock	James Pitts	John Jones
John Wendell	Stephen Greenleafe	Cornelius Waldo
William Coffin	Joshua Cheever	James Day
Harrison Gray	Thomas Jackson	Thomas Hawden
Timothy Emerson	Samuel Gardner	Henry Withered
Isaac Winslow	Thomas Gardner	John Berret
Joseph Green	Thomas Lee	Norton Quincy
Isaac Walker	Benjamin Clark	Zech. Johonnet
Edward Jackson	Joseph Green	Hopestill Foster
Ebenezer Holmes	John Turner, jun.	John Grant
William Clark	William Tyler	Charles Deming.
William Sheaffe	Samuel Bridgham	

It is hoped, That Masters and Mistresses of Family's will caution their Servants from taking in exchange or otherwise, any of said Bills if offered them, as such a thing may serve to give 'em an entrance into Credit, which would prove of dangerous consequence.

14 / The liquidation of Colman's land-bank accounts entailed complicated bookkeeping procedures.

20

nent merchant and ship owner in Boston. After losing his battle for a charter in 1714 he continued with even more determination to promote his idea. He published pamphlets and even tried to convince farmers that an increased circulation of bank notes would stimulate better prices for their crops. In 1740, after he obtained 395 signatures in 64 different Massachusetts towns supporting his petition for a private land bank, Colman's efforts were finally rewarded. He and his associates were enabled to begin issuing notes called "manufactory bills" in denominations from three pence to twenty shillings; borrowers could repay their loans in various ways, including bank notes or land.

Prohibition of Banks

Colman's hard-won success did not last long, however, for barely had he begun to enjoy his success when a group of Boston merchants

15 / *Portrait of a New England merchant of the 1700s; in their ledgers merchants kept the record of many important money transactions, including those with friends and acquaintances for whom they often acted as bankers.*

began trying to discredit him and his bank. This group aimed at forming a so-called "Silver Bank," backing its issues with silver, not land. Important Bostonians, with names such as Winslow, Bowdoin, Wells, joined the silver group. The dispute reached the governor's mansion and grew into the major political issue of the time. Eventually, Governor Jonathan Belcher denied charters to either bank and prohibited circulation of their notes, but even before Colman's bank issued any notes at all Belcher warned the populace "of the danger they are in and cautioning them against receiving or passing the said notes, as tending to defraud men of their substance, and to disturb the peace and good order of the people." The governor subjected partisans of the land bank to reprisals.

The bitter fight took such dimensions that Colman's adversaries did not hesitate to denounce

The Virginia Gazette facsimile, May 9, 1755, No. 226.

16 / "... the plan I formerly drew for a Bank, which in their opinion was the most probable means to answer our present exigencies.... Our trade seems at present to languish, and be almost expiring for want of a proper Medium to support it.... To remedy that Inconvenience I propose a Bank should be erected ... which might safely have emitted Notes...." One of the plans for a bank in Virginia in 1755.

him to the British. They asked Parliament that the so-called "Bubble Act," passed in 1720 in England to prevent speculative organizations, be extended to the Colonies. Reversing previous decisions favorable to private banks, in 1741 the English Parliament ruled that the "Bubble Act" be applied also to land banks. The pitiful play of some local rivalries had far-reaching results. The new law put a stop to all banking activities in the Colonies. Although Belcher was ultimately forced to resign in the face of protest against his policies, the Parliamentary ruling persisted until the Revolution swept it away. In retrospect, John Adams rightly remarked that "the destruction of the bank raised greater ferment in the province than the stamp-act did."

How did people transact their business during those years when there were no banks? Payments were made by actual transfer of

17 / Nathaniel Hurd (1730-77), a well-known Boston engraver, printed and sold this exchange table, a real necessity in those times of monetary confusion.

COINS	Weights oz. dwt. gr.	Value OLD TENOR	Lawfull Money
Guinea	0.5.9	10.10.—	28/
Half D.	2.16½	5.5.—	14/
Moidore	6.22	13.10.—	36/
Half D.	3.11	6.15.—	18/
Doubloon or 4 Pistole Piece	17.8	33.—	88/
Half D.	8.16	16.10.—	44/
Pistole	4.8	8.5.—	22/
Half D.	2.4	4.2.6	11/
Double Joannes or £3.12 Sterl. Piece	18.10	36.—	96/
Single Joannes or 36/ Sterl. Piece	9.5	18.—	48/
Half D.	4.14½	9.—	24/
Quarter D.	2.7¼	4.10.—	12/

ENGRAV'D. Printed & Sold by NAT. HURD.

Silver Coins	Weights oz. gr.	Value £ s d
Eng Crown	0.19.8½	2.10.—
Half Ditto	9.16½	1.5.—
Dollar	17.12	2.5.—
Half Ditto	8.18	1.2.6
Quarter D.	4.9	.11.3

N.B. 24 Grains is one penny wt. 20 Penny wt. is one Ounce.

oz. dwt. gr.	GOLD p oz. £38.0.0	SILVER p oz. 2.10.0
1.0.0	38.0.0	2.10.0
.10.0	19.—	1.5.—
.5.0	9.10.—	.12.6
2.0	3.16.—	.5.
1.0	1.18.—	.2.6
0.12	.19.—	.1.3
0.6	.9.6	0.7½
0.3	.4.9	0.3¾
0.1	.1.7	0.1¼

money from hand to hand, or without money at all, by barter. Anyone who had money wanted a safe keeping-place for it, and often turned to merchants or silversmiths, who kept strong boxes. Millers often acted as bankers for farmers, as did tavernkeepers and storekeepers in the towns. From among the large number of anonymous individuals and firms that helped the colonists manage their finances emerges one name, the Steinman Hardware Store, established in 1744 in Lancaster, Pennsylvania. For a generation the Steinmans helped their neighbors, especially the Moravians of Lititz and Lancaster, by providing safe-keeping of their cash, and even paying interest on the money.

Merchants who were used to handling money and keeping accounts abroad often fulfilled the role we expect today from banks. They extended credit, they made transfers of funds, and their surviving ledgers often bear testimony to these activities.

The Want For Banks Continues

Notwithstanding the prohibitive British laws, many colonists continued to plan for banks, and banking was a subject openly discussed in the newspapers. The *Virginia Gazette* on May 9th, 1755, carried a front page story regarding the establishment of a bank, written by Lunsford Lomax of Williamsburg at the request of "some gentlemen well versed in trade." According to contemporary thought the main purpose of a bank was to issue paper currency, and Mr. Lomax had worked out a plan for issuing up to 100,000 pounds in notes secured by capital of approximately 50,000 pounds obtained from a poll-tax and imposts on tobacco and salt. Since history has not recorded any banking venture or paper money issue connected with Lunsford

Lomax's name, we must assume that his project never progressed any further. It was another proposal for alleviating an intolerable situation, another dream.

Two years later, the same *Virginia Gazette* reported news from New York that a subscription was planned "by the principal merchants and landed gentlemen, for establishing a bank," but, again, nothing further. In May 1768, the newspaper carried a notice from London indicating that "our Gracious Sovereign is no way offended at the economy of the Americans," that "no act of Parliament suppresses your paper money," and that "you have to be relieved by having a Bank as they have in Ireland and Scotland." The notice promised that "All due attention will be paid to any petition from the people. . . ." No action followed this invitation, and soon it was lost in the gathering clouds of revolution.

Liberties, ... receive the above ...... , ... re... a le ch.rges,   JOHN SMITH.

Philadelphia, July 19 1782.

Haym Solomons,

BROKER to the Office of Finance, to the Conful General of France, and to the Treafurer of the French Army, at his Office in Front-ftreet; between Market and Arch ftreets, BUYS and SELLS on Commiffion

BANK Stock, Bills of Exchange on France, Spain, Holland, and other parts of Europe, the Weft-Indies, and inland bills, at the ufual commiffion.——He Buys and Sells

Loan-Office Certificates, Continental and State Money, of this o any other ftate, Paymafter and Quartermafter General's Notes; thefe and every other kind of paper tranfactions (bills of exchange excepted) he will charge his employers no more than ONE HALF PER CENT on his Commiffion,

He procures Money on Loan

for a fhort time, and gets Notes and Bills difcounted.

Gentlemen and others, refiding in this ftate, or any of the united ftates, by fending their orders to this Office, may depend on having their bufinefs tranfacted with as much fidelity and expedition, as if they were themfelves prefent.

He receives Tobacco, Sugars, Tea, and every other fort of Goods to Sell on Commiffion; for which purpofe he has provided proper Stores.

He flatters himfelf, his affiduity, punctuality, and extenfive connections in his bufinefs, as a Broker, is well eftablifhed in various parts of Europe, and in the united ftates in particular.

All perfons who fhall pleafe to favour him with their bufinefs, may depend upon his utmoft exertion for their intereft, and——

Part of the Money advanced, if required.

N. B. Paymafter-General's Notes taken as Cafh for Bills of Exchange.

HORSES.

The Subfcriber has removed his

HORSES to a commodious ftable in Church alley, where he has Opened a LIVERY. He pro...

18 / "He procures money on loan. . . . He buys and sells Continental and State money . . . he buys and sells on commission bank stock, bills of exchange . . . he receives tobacco, sugar, tea . . . to sell on commission." Many of these banking functions were performed by brokers. The broker Haym Solomon (1740-86), born in Poland of Jewish parentage, played an important role during the Revolution, raising money for the Continental Congress.

Local governments in the colonies, when faced with emergency expenditures such as those attendant upon General Braddock's expedition in 1755, were often forced to issue paper currencies as a temporary solution. Issued originally only with a limited scope to cover war expenditures or other emergency spendings, these bills were seldom redeemed in hard money, as promised. They depreciated rapidly and often resulted in grievous financial losses.

During the Revolution the Continental Congress had to resort to the old remedy of printing paper money. The notes, ostensibly issued only as "an anticipation" of tax revenue, began to circulate as money. As the quantity of this so-called "Continental currency" increased—old issues were not recalled when new ones were put out—depreciation inevitably resulted. Nothing Congress did could halt their rapid devaluation, and "not worth a Continental" came into our language as signifying absolute worthlessness.

In addition to the bills of the Continental Congress, each of the former colonies issued new paper money after the outbreak of the war, and its depreciation compounded the general monetary confusion. "Barber shops were papered in fact with the bills," noted a contemporary, "and sailors, on being paid off in bundles of these worthless paper money, had suits of clothes made of it."

SCALE
OF
DEPRECIATION,

Agreeable to an Act of the Commonwealth of Massachusetts to be observed as a Rule for settling the rate of Depreciation on all contracts both publick and private, made
on or since the first day of January, 1777——

One Hundred Dollars in Gold and Silver in January 1777, being equal to One Hundred and Five Dollars in the Bills of
Credit of the United States.

One thousand seven hundred and seventy-seven.

January,	105	April,	112	July,	125	October,	275
February,	107	May,	115	August,	150	November,	300
March,	109	June,	120	September,	175	December,	310

One thousand seven hundred and seventy-eight.

January,	325	April,	400	July,	425	October,	500
February,	350	May,	400	August,	450	November,	545
March,	375	June,	400	September,	475	December,	634

One thousand seven hundred and seventy-nine.

January,	742	April,	1104	July,	1477	October,	2030
February,	868	May,	1215	August,	1630	November,	2308
March,	1000	June,	1342	September,	1800	December,	2593

One thousand seven hundred and eighty.

| January, | 2934 | February, | 3322 | March, | 3736 | April, | 4000 |

From April 1st, 1780, to April 20th, one Spanish milled dollar
was equal to Forty of the old Emission.

April 25th,	42	May 20th,	54	June 20th,	69	Novem. 30th,	74
April 30th,	44	May 25th,	60	August 15th,	70	February 27th	
May 5th,	46	May 30th,	62	Septem. 10th,	71	1781,	75
May 10th,	47	June 10th,	64	October 15th,	72		
May 15th,	49	June 15th,	68	Novem. 10th,	73		

Depreciation of the New Emission.

From the 27th of February, 1781, to the 1st of May following, 1¾ of a Dollar of
the said New Emission was equal to one Dollar in Specie.
From the 1st to the 25th of May 2½ of the New Emission, equal to one in Specie.
From the 25th of May to the 15th of June, three of the New Emission for one in Specie.
From the 15th of June to the 1st of October, four of the New Emission were equal
to one in Specie.

Shaping of an Institution

21 / Robert Morris (1734-1806), the "Financier of the American Revolution." He lived up to his words: "Whatever I can do shall be done for the good of the service."

22 / George Clymer (1739-1813).

23 / The Coffee House where a group of Philadelphians gathered on June 8, 1780, to organize a bank to raise money for the Continental Army.

The Pennsylvania Bank

"A Bank to Raise Money to Supply and Transport Food to the Army"

20 / Alexander Hamilton reading the constitution of the Bank of New York *to its cofounders.*

The year 1780 started ominously. Congress had almost exhausted its resources to finance the war through lotteries or loans, while the existing paper currency continued its inexorable plunge toward complete worthlessness. The morale of the army—cold, hungry, and without pay—was low, and soldiers were often inclined to mutiny. "From the want of money, means, and credit," Thomas Paine wrote, the government "dragged on like a heavy-loaded carriage without wheels." Just as things seemed most hopeless a group of private citizens in Philadelphia decided to undertake a salvaging action.

Prominent among those Philadelphians who put their fortunes at stake in order to help the army in distress were Blair McClenach, Robert Morris, Thomas Willing, John Nixon, George Clymer, and James Wilson. On June 8, 1780, they met at the Coffee-House and

24 / John Nixon, a prominent Philadelphian, who was the second president of the Bank of North America, 1792-1808.

opened a subscription which yielded four hundred pounds in hard money and almost 1500 pounds in Continental money within a few days. More important, their gesture opened the way for a concerted action. After the loss of Charleston to the British these same men initiated a larger subscription, for 300,000 pounds; subscribers pledged their "property and credit . . . in order to support the credit of a bank to be established for furnishing a supply of provision for the armies of the United States." Robert Morris and Blair McClenach each pledged 10,000 pounds. Among the 92 sub-scribers we find also the names of George Clymer and James Wilson, signers of the Declaration of Independence, and that of Benjamin Rush, the famous physician and social reformer.

The subscribers formed an organization they named the *Pennsylvania Bank*, Robert Morris acting as one of its inspectors, and John Nixon and George Clymer as directors. Congress immediately acknowledged the Bank's offer, accepting it "as a distinguished proof of the patriotism of the subscribers." The *Pennsylvania Bank* opened for business July 7, 1780, on Front Street near Walnut, with regular office hours from nine to five. It kept its promises: its money bought flour, beef, pork, salt, sugar, rum, and other supplies for the soldiers, and when it finally wound up its affairs late in 1784 it had provided the Continental Army with some million rations.

The Establishment of a National Bank
The Bank of North America

Well intentioned as the *Pennsylvania Bank* was, it could not satisfy all the demands of a country at war. In February 1781 Robert Morris was designated Superintendent of Finance, and he immediately set about to create a national bank as "the principal pillar of American credit." Combining his vast business experience with the methodical thinking of Alexander Hamilton, Morris submitted in May of the same year to Congress, the plan for a bank capitalized at about three million dollars and closely linked to the government. Its notes, payable on demand, were to be legal tender for duties and taxes in every state of the Confederation.

The Bank's "seeds were small," as a contemporary said, public

THE Subfcribers to the *National Bank*, or their Reprefentatives, are requefted to meet at the *City Tavern*, on *Thurfday*, the firft of *November*, at at Ten o'Clock in the Forenoon, to chufe DIRECTORS.

GEORGE CLYMER,
JOHN NIXON.

25 / Ads in the local papers announced subscription meetings, as well as a dividend payment.

26 / William Bingham (1752-1804), banker and political leader in Philadelphia.

27 / The nation's first bank, the Bank of North America, *was located in this store on Chestnut Street in Philadelphia.*

28 / A present-day reconstruction of the office of the Bank of North America *in Philadelphia.*

subscriptions were slow to come in and the funds had to be supplemented with almost half a million dollars in French écus. (A shipment of specie from France was lodged in the vaults of the bank.) After a public meeting at the City Tavern in Philadelphia in November 1781, a meeting attended mostly by patrons of the *Pennsylvania Bank,* the new *Bank of North America* was launched as a national enterprise. Its president, Thomas Willing, one of Philadelphia's most distinguished and wealthy merchants, was assisted by a board of directors and seven employees. On January 7, 1782, the Bank began its operations in "a commodious store" belonging to its cashier, Tench Francis, on Chestnut Street in the heart of Philadelphia.

The Bank soon encountered serious problems. Funds and more funds were needed, since, as a contemporary said, "This sum

30

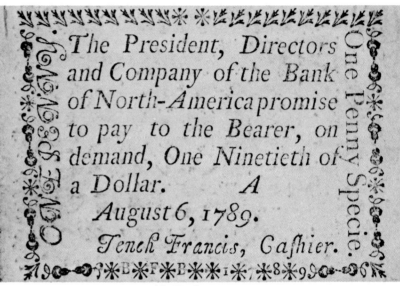

29 / A one-penny note, 1789, signed by Tench
Francis, the Bank's cashier.

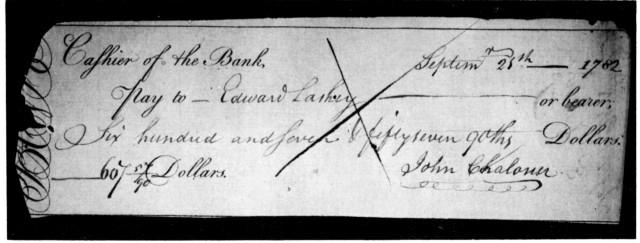

30 / This check of September 1782, drawn on the
"Bank"—the only bank then in existence, the
Bank of North America—is one of the earliest
extant checks in the United States.

31 / William Phillips (1722-1804), Boston merchant and founder of the Massachusetts Bank.

A BANK.

THE Utility of a Bank, eſtabliſhed on right Principles, being generally known and acknowledged, a Plan has been projeſted, and is now ready for the Patronage of thoſe Gentlemen who wiſh to derive the many public and private Advantages which have reſulted from ſuch Inſtitutions in other Countries.--- Copies of the Plan are lodged with, and Subſcriptions received by *William Phillips, Iſaac Smith, Jonathan Maſon, Thomas Ruſſel, John Lowell,* and *Stephen Higginſon,* Eſquires, and at the Offices of *Edward Payne, John Hurd,* and *M. M. Hays,* Eſq'rs.

32 / The Massachusetts Bank's *first announcement.*

may be said to have been paid in with one hand and borrowed with the other." Its notes were well protected, counterfeiting or passing counterfeits being a "felony without benefit of clergy." Nevertheless, painful experiences with the paper currency of the Continental Congress engendered a widespread reluctance to accept the new notes at par value; New England, for example, valued them fifteen percent below. To counteract this, bank officials attempted to strengthen its reputation by encouraging "people from the country and laboring men to go to the bank and get silver in exchange for notes." Visitors to the Bank were said to have found "a display of silver on the counter, and men employed in raising boxes containing silver, or supposed to contain silver, from the cellar to the banking-room, or lowering them from the banking-room into the cellar."

By skillful management, Morris kept the Bank operating. "Without the establishment of the national bank," he declared, "the business of the Department of Finance could not have been performed." Nevertheless, as a contemporary author stated, "the immense advantages of this institution to the credit and money-operations of the United States, as well as to the merchants, could not skreen it from popular jealousy." At one point almost 1200 people signed a petition against the Bank. It was blamed for all the economic ills of the post-Revolutionary period, and popular opposition was such that it was able to continue its existence only under a Pennsylvania state charter. During the Civil War, it received a belated recognition. When reorganized as a national bank in 1864 it was the only bank not required to include the word "National" in its name.

31

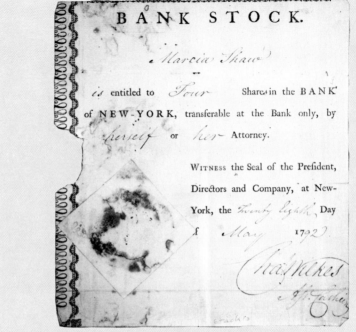

33 / *Initial stock certificate of the* Bank of New York, 1792.

34-35 / *Two checks drawn on the* Bank of New York, *signed by Baron von Steuben and by Aaron Burr, Hamilton's great adversary.*

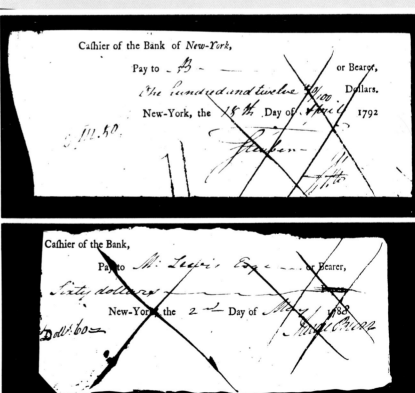

36 | *Alexander Hamilton, who drew up the bank's articles of association.*

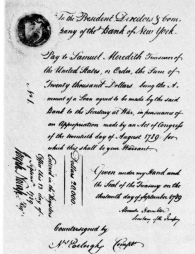

37 | *United States Treasury Warrant No. 1 for $20,000 signed by Alexander Hamilton, drawn on the* Bank of New York.

38 | *The bank's building since 1797, at Wall and William Streets.*

The Massachusetts Bank

On New Year's Day, 1784, the Boston *Independent Chronicle* announced that "The utility of a bank, established on right principles, being generally known and acknowledged, a plan has been projected, and is now ready for the patronage of those gentlemen who wish to derive the many public and private advantages." After getting advice and guidance from Thomas Willing, President of the *Bank of North America,* six Bostonians, including a wealthy merchant named William Phillips, had petitioned for a state charter. The *Massachusetts Bank,* as the new bank was named, was closely patterned after the Philadelphia Bank. Both kept their accounts in Mexican dollars. "The world is apt to suppose a greater mystery in this sort of business, than there really is; perhaps it is right they should do so," was Willing's advice to

his Boston friends. To be initiated into "this mystery" of banking, the accountant of the Boston bank spent some time in Philadelphia studying methods of bookkeeping.

The mentor of the Bank, William Phillips (1722-1804), was a wholesale trader whose main characteristics a contemporary described as "formality and a Presbytherian face." It is perhaps also worth mentioning that Phillips was one of only twenty-one Bostonians to own a carriage before the Revolution. A member of the Continental Congress, Samuel Osgood, was the Bank's first cashier, the distinguished James Bowdoin its first president.

The Bank of New York

In New York, Robert R. Livingston and other gentry had once tried to organize a land bank, but they failed to win the support of the New York City merchants. Then,

34

40 | *A figure of a river god labeled "public health" on this five dollar note issued by the* Manhattan Company *in 1813.*

on February 23, 1784, the *New York Packet* carried a notice referring to "the disposition of the gentlemen in this city, to establish a Bank on liberal principles, the stock to consist of specie only." Interested persons were invited "to meet to-morrow evening at six o'clock at the Merchants' Coffee House."

The driving force behind the newly organized *Bank of New York* was Alexander Hamilton. He helped write its constitution and then became one of its directors. Hamilton wanted the capital, $500,000, to be subscribed in gold or silver only. Most of this consisted of Spanish, Portuguese, German, French, and English gold coins, and French silver écus.

The Bank initially commenced business in the Walton Mansion at 11 Hanover Street, then in 1798 moved to permanent quarters at 48 Wall Street. Before it moved, its president, Isaac Roosevelt, en-

41 / *Fifty dollar note issued by the* Bank of Pennsylvania.

joyed the convenience of attending to his own business, a sugar-refinery, just across the street, before performing his duties as president of the bank.

The *Bank of New York,* one of the nation's important financial institutions, still prides itself in having been the first bank to make a loan to the new federal government in 1789.

The Manhattan Company

One of the richest of New York's early banks, the *Manhattan Company,* which began operation in September 1799, owed its existence to a clever scheme perpetrated by Aaron Burr. Burr knew he had no chance to obtain a banking charter, since the New York state legislature was under the influence of Alexander Hamilton, Secretary of the Treasury, and also a director of the *Bank of New York.* So Burr resorted to a subterfuge; he applied for a charter for

42 / *The* Bank of Pennsylvania *located on Second Street between Chestnut and Walnut was one of B. H. Latrobe's greatest works done in white marble in imitation of the ancient Temple of the Muses near Athens.*

43 / *Ten dollar bank note issued by the* Bank of Columbia *in Georgetown, then in Maryland, in June 1807.*

a water company. Because New York was then desperately in need of a better water supply, he was certain to get strong public support for such a project. Indeed, it is said that even his arch-enemy Hamilton spoke favorably of it. The bill Burr proposed included a clause which permitted surplus capital to be used "in the purchase of public or other stock, or in any other moneyed transactions or operations." Although this clause had been debated, nobody seems to have realized that Burr had in mind to form a bank, and the bill passed easily.

Burr's *Manhattan Company* was initially capitalized at half a million dollars; within two years this was increased to two million, double the capital of its rival, the *Bank of New York*. Burr did not neglect his water project: a contemporary publication reported that "the water-works were begun in the spring of 1799 and at the close of the year 1801, conductpipes . . . had been laid within the city to the extent of twenty miles."

The Bank of the United States

The war of the Revolution left the country deeply in debt both at home and abroad, and this situation persisted during the Confederation period. To strengthen the finances of the new Constitutional Union was the main goal of the first Secretary of the Treasury, Alexander Hamilton. In January 1790 he outlined to Congress the advantages of good public credit: "To furnish new resources both to agriculture and commerce; to

44 / *Bank note issued by the* Providence Bank *in 1812.*

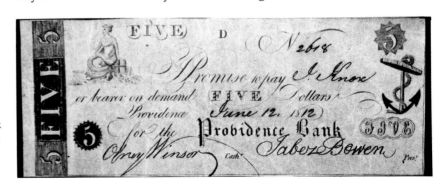

45 / *Original charter of the* Providence Bank, *signed by Arthur Fenner, Governor of Rhode Island, October 1791.*

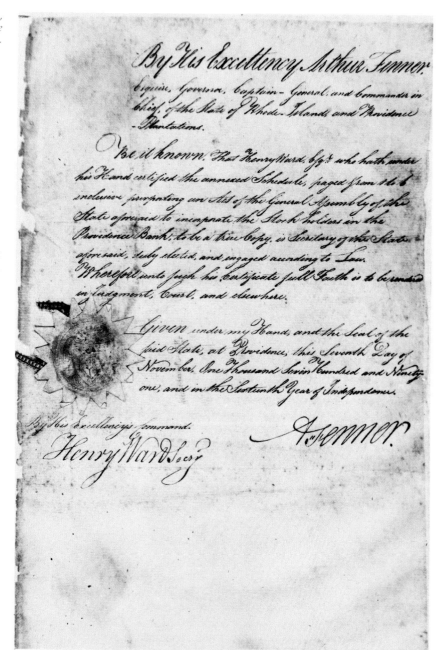

37

cement more closely the union of the States; to add to their security against foreign attacks; to establish public order."

Hamilton insisted that only a national bank, unhampered by local interests or jeopardized by unstable state legislatures, was adequate to the task at hand. Only a national bank could be truly effective in "the augmentation of the active or productive capital of a country," and in enabling the government to obtain "necessary pecuniary aid." "Mere local institutions," he insisted, "cannot serve as engines of a general circulation. For this they have neither sufficient capital, nor have they enough of the confidence of all parts of the Union." Neither was the *Bank of North America* adequate since it had lost its power and independence through restrictions imposed in its state charter.

Hamilton's plan for a national

46 / *The grandeur of the building of the first Bank of the United States was enhanced by a monumental entrance in neoclassic style by Samuel Blodget.*

47 / *The stock subscription books were opened on July 4, 1791, in Carpenter's Hall in Philadelphia. Within two hours 24,000 shares were bid in, more than the set limit.*

bank is a classic state paper. In it he clearly established many of the basic principles of American public finance. But although his ideas were fundamental in outlining the banking system of the new nation, it also embodied some concepts that were bound to be controversial, and it generated an immediate opposition. Whether or not to vest one national bank with power over the financial policies of the entire nation remained a perennial political issue. Periodically the idea would surface, but not until the 20th century did a centrally directed banking system finally lose its controversial character.

In 1791, the strongest opposition came from Thomas Jefferson. An inveterate adversary of banks, Jefferson once declared that they were more dangerous than standing armies. He considered a national bank as simply a moneyed monopoly of no general benefit.

Be it enacted by the Senate and House of Representatives of the United States of America, in Congress assembled,

Jefferson also argued from constitutional premises, pointing out that nowhere was Congress specifically empowered to establish such a bank. After a fierce political battle Hamilton succeeded in getting his bank bill through Congress, but when it came before George Washington for his signature the President requested written opinions regarding its constitutionality from Hamilton, from Secretary of State Jefferson, and from Edmund Randolph, the Attorney General. Some said that the Bank owed its existence to Hamilton's brilliant argument. He convinced the President that the Bank was indeed constitutional, on the basis of that document's "implied powers"—that Congress had "a right to employ all the means requisite and fairly applicable to the attainment of constitutional ends." Eventually the constitutionality of the Bank was confirmed by the Supreme Court.

With Washington's signature, the *Bank of the United States* was officially empowered to begin operation. It was to have a capital stock of ten million dollars divided into 25,000 shares of $400 each, one-quarter of which had to be paid in coin. The subscription books were opened in July 1791 in Carpenter's Hall in Philadelphia. The reaction was unprecedented. Within hours the subscription limit was surpassed and shares began commanding speculative prices. Express runners were paid as much as $150 to rush stock from one city to another.

Thomas Willing resigned his position as president of the *Bank of North America* to become the Bank's first president. It prospered from the very beginning and soon branch offices were established in other cities, from Boston and New York in the North to Savannah and New Orleans in the South.

The dignity of the Bank's central office in Philadelphia was symbolized by its imposing, temple-like facade. As years passed, however, considerable rivalry developed between the central bank and the growing state-chartered banks. Local resentments especially came to the fore in 1811, when Congress debated whether or not to renew the Bank's twenty-year charter. Even though the Secretary of the Treasury, Albert Gallatin, strongly recommended renewal, it was defeated by one single vote. In the words of a contemporary writer pleased by the vote, the Bank had "had its youth, its middle age, and now comes on its old age, and on the 4th of March next it will be its dissolution."

The Expansion of Banks

The creation of the *Bank of the United States* in 1791 had a catalytic effect. All over the country

48 / *Alexander Hamilton, Secretary of the Treasury, the driving force behind the* Bank of the United States.

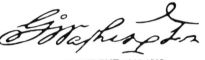

PRESIDENT 1789-1797

40

50 / *Edmund Randolph, Attorney General.*

49 / *Thomas Jefferson, Secretary of State.*

there had been a long-felt need for banks which would not only assist merchants to manage their funds, but also create credit and help the farmer, the settler, the small trader, the mechanic, and the inventor to be more productive. The year 1791 saw the creation of the *Providence Bank* chartered by the State of Rhode Island. In 1792 and 1793 other state-chartered banks followed in quick succession: the *Bank of Pennsylvania,* then banks in Albany, Charleston, Portsmouth, Alexandria, New London, New Haven, and Salem. In the same year a second bank opened in Boston, the *Union Bank.* The *Bank of Columbia* was founded in 1792 in Georgetown, then part of Maryland. It could pride itself in having George Washington among its stockholders. In his will Washington left 170 shares in the *Bank of Columbia,* as well as twenty-five in the *Bank of Alexandria.*

51 / *Thomas Willing (1731-1821), well known Philadelphia merchant, who resigned as president of the* Bank of North America *for the more prestigious position as president of the* Bank of the United States.

52 / *The bank introduced private checks which have (to the left) a scroll-pattern characteristic of indentured documents.*

53 / *Handwritten check drawn on the* Bank of the United States, 1796, *signed by Timothy Pickering, Secretary of State.*

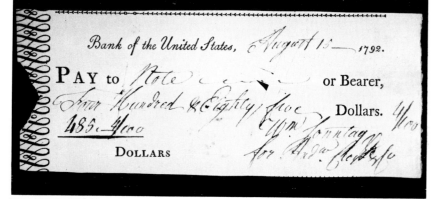

Most of these banks fulfilled each of the three different functions expected of a bank in those days: "that of issuing bills of credit commonly called bank notes; that of receiving deposits and that of loaning money at interest or discount." In order to issue bills which had the same value as specie, good credit was essential. Many Americans did strongly oppose the issuance of paper notes based on unstable assets, but others believed that "in our national credit, if we sedulously cherish and wisely employ it, we have an immense treasure, which can perform all that gold performs."

It is interesting how the early banks were organized. After electing their officials, the directors set salaries for the employees. Pay depended, of course, on the size and location of the bank. The cashier was the highest paid, often drawing as much as two

thousand dollars annually, while
the president might receive between fifteen and seventeen hundred dollars; the first teller, eight
hundred; the bookkeeper and the
discount clerk, six hundred each;
the runner, five hundred; the
porter, two hundred; and the
watchman, a hundred and fifty
dollars a year.

In the cashier's care were also
placed the plates for printing bank
notes, and he had to make provisions for this operation, usually
in the basement. One of the big-
gest problems facing all banks was
the forgery of checks and the
counterfeiting of notes. The for-

54 / *Away from the big cities, business was often
transacted in smaller, more modest buildings like
this bank in Wyoming, Pennsylvania.*

55 / *The* Philadelphia Bank *(1809) was another
of architect Latrobe's master works designed in
Gothic style. Its rooms in brick and marble were
twenty feet high with ornate ceilings. In the
cellar was the printing office for the notes.*

56 / *Nathaniel Rochester (1752-1831), banker and founder of the city of Rochester in New York.*

43

57 / *Alexander Brown (1764-1834), was a linen merchant from Ireland who founded a banking house with worldwide connections.*

mer was infrequent, but the latter had been a major plague from the very beginning, and grew steadily as the number of banks increased. An 1818 newspaper reported that it appeared "quite reasonable to believe that not many less than ten thousand persons, paper makers, engravers, signers, etc., wholesale dealers and retailers of counterfeit money, are wholly or in part engaged in swindling the honest people of the United States." During the early 19th century, this problem became so serious that banks in Philadelphia, New York, and Baltimore formed protective unions and spent large amounts to detect and apprehend counterfeiters.

But counterfeit bills were certainly not the only source of difficulty. Around 1815 a French visitor wrote: "Imagine then two hundred and forty-six classes of paper money, circulating side by side having all degrees of value,

according to the good or bad credit of the bank which issued them, at 20 percent, 30 percent, or 50 percent discount. Gold and silver had entirely disappeared, there was no longer any standard of price and value."

The refusal of Congress to renew the charter of the *Bank of the United States* was labeled an "unwise" and "woefully pernicious measure" by "A Virginian" who published a pamphlet on the *Present State of Banking Operations* in 1818. While anonymous, his account is invaluable, since it grew out of his personal experiences after the Bank's charter lapsed. "Numerous banks," he wrote, "without solidity of capital, or prudence of management sprung into existence in every part of the nation. . . . A bank was the panacea for every real or imaginary evil. . . . Nothing, therefore, became more easy than to establish a bank. . . . Specie not being required, en-

abled these banks to lend sums far exceeding not only their real but nominal capital, and thereby to produce enormous profits."

The "Virginian" continued with a vivid picture of how it all happened: "How did these projectors

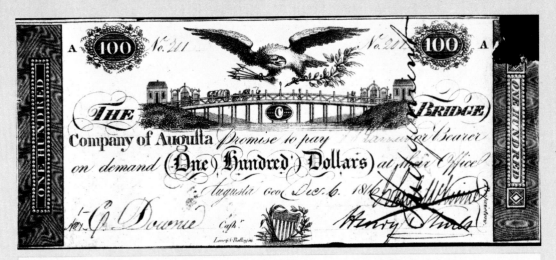

58 / In the fast-developing nation, the companies that built turnpikes and bridges often had banking authority, too; the notes served to pay employees and suppliers.

59 / To meet the needs for money and credit in a growing nation, various states chartered banks. Between 1790 and 1806 the number of banks increased from 3 to 68.

60 / The Miami Exporting Company and Bank in Cincinnati was one of the earliest banks in the new western territories and states, opening in 1803. This one dollar note was issued in 1841.

61 / *Coins, whenever available, were weighed on similar scales.*

62 / *A mallet with a raised cross for cancelling checks.*

63 / *A watchman's rattle.*

64 / *One of the most important items of banks besides ledgers were strong boxes, often fitted with a secret lock.*

go to work? They opened subscription books requiring about a twentieth part of the capital to be paid in specie, or the notes of some existing bank . . . ; the stock is taken; the officers are appointed; a banking-house is purchased, or hired; plates to make the notes intended to be issued are provided, and the bank goes into operation. . . . Stockholders . . . might receive a dividend of eight, ten, or twelve per centum per annum, not only on the capital paid in, but on the nominal capital not paid in."

The author here recommended that banks be allowed to transact business only on their nominal capital and not on some pledged amount which might never materialize. He went on to lament that "This unnecessary multiplication of banks spreads over the country an odious system of espionage, for it is notorious that . . . it is made the duty of the directors of these institutions, to inquire into, to pry into, and to know the length of every man's purse who may apply for accommodation, not only his but that of his endorser."

Finally, he concluded by asserting the indispensibility of a national bank and "a paper universal in its circulation, and certain in its value, as certain as human foresight and wisdom can make a thing." "We shall then have but one paper medium, with the stamp of the nation on it . . . —of a stable value—universal in its circulation." A national bank and a safe and universal paper currency, he insisted, would not interfere with any rights of individuals or individual states. Indeed, such a bank, with branches in every state, would "afford to merchants and all other persons the most essential accommodations . . . Such a bank, therefore, will move like the sun, shedding its blessings equally on all to whom its rays may extend." So spoke a staunch proponent of central banking in the year 1818!

66 | *The famous Tontine Coffee House (second from left) on Wall Street housed the Stock Exchange for many years.*

Banking in a Growing Nation, 1815-1860

65 | *Bank note designs reflected the progress of the country.*
◄

Financing by Many

The founding of the *Bank of the United States* in 1791 greatly stimulated interest in the ownership of bank stock, thus contributing directly to the creation of the New York Stock Exchange. The first meetings in 1792 were informal gatherings under a buttonwood tree at 68 Wall Street. Not until 1817 was the New York Stock & Exchange Board formally established and a constitution written.

The period when the nation's first banks were organized was also the formative era for its savings and trust institutions and an era of expansion for its insurance companies, each of which performed some of the functions of banks. The oldest among them were the insurance companies, which were operating in the Colonies since 1736. Their main purpose was to underwrite fire and maritime losses, but they also loaned money. Prior to 1863 many

47

67 | *A two-dollar note of the* Mississippi Marine & Fire Insurance Company, *issued in Chicago.*

68 / *Condy Raguet, a Philadelphia journalist, was the founder of the* Philadelphia Savings Fund Society.

69 / *Thomas Eddy, organized a* Bank for Savings *in New York in 1818.*

48

70 / *The bee-hive, denoting thrift, was used as its symbol.*

71 / *Savings institutions contributed to the increase in the amount of paper currency.*

insurance companies issued paper notes.

Savings societies were first patterned after Scottish and English examples. The earliest was organized in 1816 by a journalist named Condy Raguet as the *Philadelphia Savings Fund Society*. One of the main purposes of such organizations was to help the poor combat alcoholism by promoting thrift. Depositors were of all sorts: a Connecticut savings society had twice as many female as male depositors, more than 900 children under 12 years, but relatively few — only 51 — Blacks. Thomas Eddy, a well-known New York prison reformer, organized the *Bank for Savings* in 1818. Savings institutions issued numerous paper notes, especially during the crisis years of 1837 and 1857. The same was true of trust companies, but these were not formally organized until the mid 19th century.

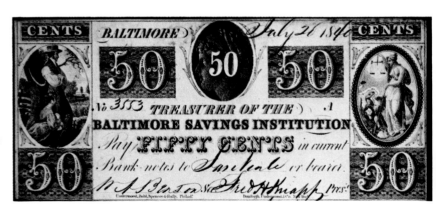

73 / *The banker Stephen Girard, an engraving after an original painting by Chappel, mid-19th century.*

Stephen Girard, Merchant and Banker of Philadelphia 1750-1831

Stephen Girard, a native of France, settled in Philadelphia in 1776, where he became a prosperous merchant and developed a fleet of ships which plied the European and West Indian trade. Girard pledged his accumulating wealth to his adopted country. In 1810, he tried to shore-up the *Bank of the United States* by investing one million dollars in its depreciated stock. When Congress refused to extend the Bank's charter in 1811, Girard bought its Philadelphia building and started a private bank bearing his own name, *The Bank of Stephen Girard*.

During the War of 1812, when the country's credit and resources were extremely low, Girard subscribed five million dollars to the war loan of 1814, about 95 percent of the total.

Even though he was a private banker, Girard gave his full support to the establishment of the second *Bank of the United States* in 1816. He helped write the charter for this new federal bank, subscribed more than anyone else— three million dollars—and became one of its first directors.

Girard became a legend during his own lifetime and numerous anecdotes are still told about this strange, lonely man. Public service

49

72 / *View of Philadelphia in the early 1800s showing the Merchants' Exchange and, in the background, the* Girard Bank *with its temple-like architecture.*

74 / The architect William Strickland invested the second Bank of the United States with the grace and dignity of the Pantheon. Surrounding the picture are portraits of men involved in the chartering of the second Bank of the United States: its supporters, James Madison, John Calhoun and Henry Clay; and two of its directors, Stephen Girard and Jacob Astor. Daniel Webster opposed the chartering of the Bank but later became one of its defenders.

became his guiding ideal. In his will he bequeathed his fortune to the public, the bulk going towards founding his school for male orphans, *Girard College*. Strangely enough, his name is perpetuated by a bank he did not found, for his own bank was liquidated after his death.

The Second Bank of the United States

The *Bank of the United States* closed its doors in 1811; politically, it had become as undesirable to the majority in Congress as it had been to most of the state and private banks. With no central bank the country was in a deplorable financial situation to go to war, and before the War of 1812 ended it had learned a lesson: as a contemporary put it, the new state banks "afforded very little support to our finances," and their credit was "too limited to afford a general circulating medium."

Many saw salvation in reviving the defunct national bank, and in 1814, merchants from New York began petitioning for its recharter. President Madison's Secretary of the Treasury, Alexander J. Dallas, kept insisting that a national bank was essential to obtaining loans for maintaining the war effort. Yet, for all the support, plus the support of political leaders such as John C. Calhoun, attempts to recharter the Bank failed on five separate occasions.

Once the war was over the emphasis changed; people wanted a bank which could settle the peacetime currency problems. Finally, on the seventh attempt, the bill passed both houses and President Madison signed a twenty-year charter for the second *Bank of the United States* in April 1816.

At the beginning the Bank was quite ineffectual in restraining the rapid increase in the number of state banks—from 88 in 1811 to 307 in 1820. Their notes helped to stimulate vast land speculations, but inevitably it all had to come to a halt. In 1818 a severe recession set in and numerous banks failed. This reopened old debates about the pros and cons of state banks versus a national bank, debates accompanied by numerous pamphlets. "Immoderate and abrupt loans foster and encourage speculation, luxury and extravagance," read one. "An ill-managed bank operates as a blast, a blight, a mildew, a sirocco. . . . It is not improbable that this nation has suffered more injury by the mis-

75 / *The graceful office of the branch bank at Savannah, completed by architect William Jay in 1823.*

management of the banks, since the war, then during the war from the enemy." Others extolled the virtues of a national bank "resting on a stable foundation" with "universal credit." Some pamphleteers sought a bank headquartered in Washington, not Philadelphia: "What is the District of Columbia?" one asked. "Is it a wilderness? Is it filled with savages and wild beasts? . . . Has nature made anywhere a finer seat for commerce?" But despite that writer's rhetoric, Washington remained with only a branch of the Bank, one of twenty-eight distributed over an area from Maine to Georgia to Missouri.

The Rapid Growth of Banks

Soon after the first banks opened, it became clear that paper money was no panacea. Many people expected to have notes paid in metallic currency any time, while banks tried to avoid this because

specie was often in short supply. Sometimes unscrupulous speculators started banks on very shaky foundations. Some bankers tried to circulate their notes far away from their bank. These so-called "saddle-bag" banks employed traveling agents to loan out their money.

Americans simply lacked confidence in paper money. Various debacles of Colonial and Revolutionary times were still a fresh memory; the slightest suspicion about the value of a bank's paper could set off a panic. In a rapidly growing nation speculation was inevitable, and a small amount of bad money mingled with good could contaminate it all.

News traveled fast and people were ready to believe the worst, even though the great majority of bankers were honest and dedicated men. A French traveler noted that "Hatred of speculators and, through association, of the bank-

ing system had taken root in the hearts of the mass of the people." Yet, he also saw that banks had "served the Americans as a lever to transport to their soil . . . the agriculture and manufactures of Europe and to cover their country with roads, canals, factories, schools, churches. . . ." Banks, he added, had enabled the American "to cultivate lands which are now in his hands worth tenfold or a hundredfold." This was indeed true, especially of banks in the West. In Illinois, for example, banks were regarded as "powerful engines for the painless provision" of capital. In the words of one writer, the chief function of western banks "seems to have been to manufacture paper money and issue it on easy terms to the ambitious but impecunious inhabitants."

Companies formed to build canals, turnpikes, and railroads sought banking privileges to free

76 / In response to skyrocketing demands for credit, banks mushroomed everywhere, and sales of bank shares boomed.

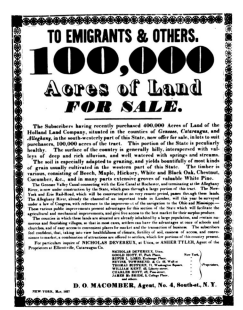

77 / The nation was involved in one of the wildest land speculations ever.

them from the exigencies of raising capital. After having come through hard times in 1819, Americans were again eager to invest in profitable ventures. At Philadelphia in 1821, the entire stock of the Union Canal was subscribed within fifteen minutes. The number of banks was also growing by leaps and bounds, as was the number of individuals with bank holdings. Of special interest in the latter regard was the steady increase in bank holdings by women. In the *Massachusetts Bank* in Boston, for example, their number grew from 30 in 1784, to 336 in 1810, to 577 in 1825.

What did a bank look like in those days? We have many descriptions of luxurious East Coast institutions, with lavish marble steps leading to richly ornamented offices. In contrast to the plentiful information about such "halls of marvel," however, only rarely can we get a glimpse of a more modest

bank. Still, a few descriptions do exist, such as this generalized one of small-town banks in Iowa in the 1850s: "The office was generally in a cheap and ordinary one-story frame or brick building with few doors and windows. The building consisted of one and sometimes two rooms. In the front room, a plain, wide counter of pine or black walnut separated a banker from his customer. Little furniture was found in these early banks: in general a couple of chairs, a stove, a table, and a standing desk were sufficient. There were no individual cages for each employee, for often there was but one man who was the president, cashier, teller, bookkeeper, and janitor. Neither were there mahogany furnished waiting rooms for the comfort of the bank's customers. Everyone who wished to sit down might use the counter as a seat."

Bankers whose businesses were

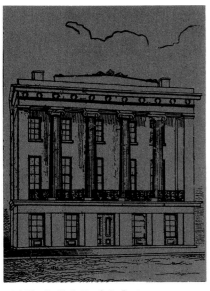

78 / The Suffolk Bank in Boston.

79-80 / The stamps BROKEN BANK or WORTHLESS were often used by the Suffolk Bank.

81 / Joshua Forman (1777-1848), lawyer and originator of the New York Safety System.

attached to their homes were advised that "the building should be so constructed that what is going on in the private house, whether in the kitchen, or the nursery, or the drawing room, should not be heard in the bank." It would have been difficult to adhere to this in a small-town bank, where the banker might be loaning money in the front room while his wife fried eggs for dinner in the back!

The metallistic aspect of money was so pronounced in the mid-19th century that specie was used as a sort of magic tranquilizer. A Connecticut banker, we are told, ostentatiously exhibited an open chest filled with silver coins in order to buoy-up the confidence of customers to whom he was loaning paper money. An even stranger thing happened in Illinois, where a bank that had been robbed of its specie took in two lone silver dollars and then promptly put them on exhibit!

Of course, sometimes and in some places specie was plentiful. A hilarious anecdote published in the 1860s concerned an individual who had been refused a loan by a certain bank. A few days later he came back with a $40,000 bundle of that bank's notes, asking to be paid in specie. He got his request. The paying teller had the coins rolled out to him in kegs of one thousand dollars each, apologizing for having to pay him in five- and ten-cent pieces. But the customer was not to be outsmarted. He opened every single keg and took a handful of coins from each. Then he turned ever so nonchalantly to the teller and asked him to place the remainder on account. Of course, the teller had to count the coins one by one. The only thing the story does not tell is how the customer ever managed to withdraw his deposit.

A very real problem to anybody who handled paper money was counterfeits, a bugaboo since colonial times when bills carried

53

82 / *Nicholas Biddle (1786-1844), the aristocratic head of the* Bank of the United States.

83 / *Henry Clay (1777-1857), Senator from Kentucky, an adamant supporter of the Bank.*

the warning: "Death to the counterfeiter." Presumably that was a threat seldom carried out. In the 1830s some bank officials tried to protect themselves against losses by docking the hapless cashier for any sums paid out for counterfeits, but that solution must have been none too satisfactory either. The best protection against counterfeits was a sharp eye: Jay Cooke, the famous banker of the Civil War period and after, took pride in his ability to spot a counterfeit note from several feet away, and averred as to how this was a major secret of his success.

Finally, a contemporary describes a good teller in action: "A bank teller requires an instinctive faculty for the detection of spurious bills. To stand by and observe him counting, it might be supposed that he can hardly get a glimpse of each so rapidly do they pass through his hands . . . there goes one aside without perceptible pause in the handling. He checks the item on the list and with his right hand thrusts the pile into a drawer, whilst with the left he tosses the single bill to the depositor. — 'Counterfeit — five dollars off! . . . Where did you get that altered bill?' he asks the customer, meanwhile counting — twenty, thirty, fifty, fifty-five, sixty."

A teller had to be endowed not only with a very perceptive eye but also with an impeccable memory. Some spurious bills were printed from perfectly genuine plates, their only shortcoming being that the issuing bank was defunct. Once in a while an engraver who had failed sold his plates to a forger, who then

84 / *The central office of the second* Bank of the United States *in Philadelphia.*

85 / *Andrew Jackson (1767-1845), President of the United States who decided to put an end to the power of the Bank.*

86 / *Roger B. Taney (1777-1864), Attorney General and the President's chief counselor in the war against the Bank.*

87 / *William J. Duane (1780-1865), Secretary of the Treasury who resigned rather than carry out Jackson's orders regarding the Bank.*

provided bills with fake names, signatures, and numbers.

The first serious attempt to dam the flood of worthless notes was made by the *Suffolk Bank* in Boston. Its name can be seen stamped in black ink on various bills, along with the bold imprint, WORTH-LESS or COUNTERFEIT. Beginning in 1819 the *Suffolk Bank* acted as a self-appointed controlling and regulating authority. It offered to redeem at par all notes of any bank anywhere in the country, so long as it had deposited a redemption fund with the *Suffolk Bank.* Many banks in New England did so, and this group of healthy financial institutions became an important stabilizing factor in the nation's economy. Notes accepted by the *Suffolk Bank* automatically gained general respect.

A counterpart to the *Suffolk Bank* was the *Metropolitan Bank* in New York City. In 1829 Joshua Forman (1777-1848), a lawyer and promoter of the Erie Canal, developed a bank safety and insurance system, and New York subsequently became known as a bulwark of sound banking. Forman's system required every new bank to pay a certain amount into a central fund, which could be drawn upon to cover any liabilities in case of a bank failure. The Safety Fund idea soon spread to other states: Vermont (1831), Indiana (1834), Michigan (1836), and Ohio (1845).

The Central Bank Becomes a Major Political Issue

"I do not dislike your Bank," President Andrew Jackson once told Nicholas Biddle, the head of the *Bank of the United States,* "any more than all banks. But ever since I read the history of the South Sea Bubble, I have been afraid of banks." These words scarcely suggest the passion with which Jackson fought the Bank. It was a contest which overshadowed all other political battles of the time. It was a contest which involved not only the two personal adversaries and the two political parties, the Democrats and the National Republicans (or Whigs), but also agitated the entire nation.

The contest focused on the question of renewing the charter of the *Bank of the United States,* which was due to expire in 1836. Above all it was a clash of personalities: Nicholas Biddle, the aristocratic, dashing, bright, and very ambitious head of the Bank and representative of the moneyed interests; and Andrew Jackson, the hot-tempered, autocratic man of the people, the Democrat who deeply distrusted centralized power. To Jackson the Bank was a dangerous monopoly whose paper currency "drove from circulation the constitutional currency." "Constitutional currency" to him

88 / Popular sentiments regarding that bitter
war on the Bank were often expressed in merciless
satire in cartoons, tokens, or "fun money."

89 / Martin Van Buren, successor to Jackson in the Presidency, relied more on "hard" money than on bank credit.

meant gold and silver. He thought that paper currency "engendered a spirit of speculation injurious to the habits and character of people," and that it fostered an "eager desire to amass wealth without labor."

Jackson seems to have been insufficiently attentive to the scarcity of metallic currency and to the monetary needs of a rapidly growing nation. But even if his general ideas were correct, his attacks were misdirected, since the main offenders were the state banks with their plethora of notes. In fact, in this regard the *Bank of the United States* had always exerted a restraining influence.

To the basic ideas which had held sway among the Democrats since Thomas Jefferson's time, Jackson added a deep personal dislike for the Bank, for Biddle, and for many of the Bank's ardent supporters, such as his arch-rival, Henry Clay. The irony is that Jackson's attack was launched just as the Bank was on the verge of becoming a genuine

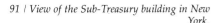

90 / This token expresses a popular feeling that the Sub-Treasury system was ineffective and slow as a "turtle."

91 / View of the Sub-Treasury building in New York.

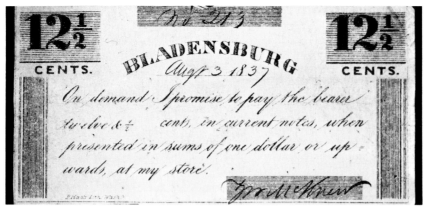

92 / In the year of panic, 1837, "shinplasters," privately issued fractional notes, replaced "hard" money rendered scarce by the suspension of specie by the banks.

asset to the nation. Under the capable direction of Biddle, it was bringing some semblance of stability to the currency by reducing the growth of state banks and assuring that those which stayed in business were solvent. Its own assets were certainly good, for when it was forced to close it showed a considerable surplus of funds in spite of heavy losses caused by its fight to stay alive.

That fight had begun in 1831 when Biddle—acting on Clay's advice—petitioned Congress for a new charter well in advance of the original charter's expiration date in 1836. Both houses approved the recharter but Andrew Jackson vetoed it. In the presidential campaign of 1832 the Bank became the overriding issue. Jackson's electoral victory sealed the fate of the Bank.

Next, Jackson ordered the removal of all federal funds from the Bank, and their deposit in certain

93 / Nathaniel Currier, the famous lithographer, drew his caricature of a "wild-cat banker," and cartoonists ridiculed the notorious "wild-cat" banks which "amounted to a handful of straw."

selected state banks. These were soon labeled "pet banks." After that the conflict escalated, with vicious attacks and counter-attacks on both Biddle and the President. A leading politician remarked that it would "be difficult for people in after times to realize the degree of excitement, of agitation, and of commotion which was produced by this organized attempt to make panic and distress. The great cities especially were the scene of commotions but little short of frenzy." Newspapers were warning that "the clangor of arms and the voice of battle" would soon "resound in the land." Epithets were flying both ways, with the President denouncing the Bank as a "monster" and a "hydra," and his enemies calling him a "tyrant," a "usurper," an "infatuated old man," and a "Cromwell." Cartoonists depicted Biddle, "Emperor Nicholas," with horns, hooves, and tail. The cry "blood must flow" was heard, the people exhorted to break Jackson's "despotism." Jackson even declared that he would "seek an asylum in the wilds of Arabia" before he would allow recharter of the "monster."

Behind Jackson was his Attorney General, Roger B. Taney, an uncompromising man who drove the President to fight on. One casualty was William J. Duane, Secretary of the Treasury, who was dismissed in September 1833 rather than carry out the President's order to remove federal funds from the Bank. This he considered a vindictive move, as he explained in his letter of resignation: "Solemnly impressed with a profound sense of my obligations to my country . . . I respectfully announce to you, Sir, that I refuse to carry your directions into effect. . . . Because I consider the proposed change . . . a breach of the public faith." He closed by saying to Jackson, "I feel a sorrow on your account, far greater than on my own."

Duane predicted that ". . . a change to local and irresponsible banks will tend to shake public confidence, and promote doubt and mischief in the operations of society." These prophetic words foretold a disaster in the offing, a period indelibly inscribed in the nation's history as the "Hard Times," the panic and depression which began in 1837.

The Proliferation of Banks and Bank Notes Before the Civil War

"We Want Good Money"

Jackson's attack on the *Bank of the United States* and the distribution of its government deposits among state banks fostered great uncertainty in the business world. Nevertheless, these were also boom years. The sale of western lands increased four hundred times between 1830 and 1836, while the

BANKS AND THE COUNTRY'S ENTERPRISES

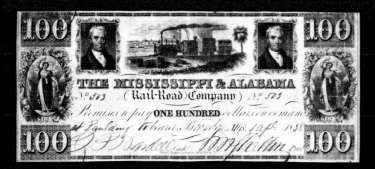

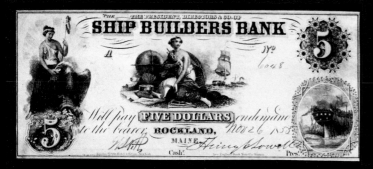

94 / Banks were intimately involved in the country's tremendous growth during the first half of the 1800s and they helped finance many significant enterprises. Pride in their contributions to the nation's achievements found expression in the pictorial representations on bank notes. The names of many banks are indicative of the industrial enterprises they catered to, such as turnpikes, canals, railroads, or shipyards.

MANUFACTURE OF BANKNOTES

95 | Jacob Perkins (1766-1849), a well-known bank note manufacturer and inventor, and a note engraved in his characteristic style intended to discourage counterfeiting.

96 | Asher B. Durand (1796-1886), a noted printer and engraver, and note produced by him.

97 | The American Bank Note Company of New York produced some of the finest bank notes.

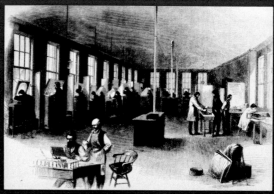

98 | In the letter engraving room, artists hand-engraved numerals and letters.

99 | The pictorial engraving room where images like these, called "vignettes," were engraved.

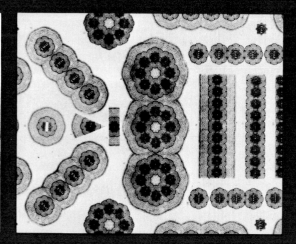

100 | Skilled machinists produced intricate rosettes on a geometrical lathe, intended to render the counterfeiting of notes impossible.

101 / In the paper wareroom meticulous attention was given to the storage of bank-note paper.

103 / The finished steel or copper plates were kept under special care.

102 / In the printing room where many presses were at work, each color was printed separately.

104 / The ink-mill: because of counterfeiting, the chemical composition of inks was very important.

number of banks almost doubled. Hugh McCulloch, at the time a banker in Indiana, though later Lincoln's Secretary of the Treasury, decried not only the war on the Bank, but the whole contemporary situation: "It is not difficult to discover the causes of the great financial troubles . . . (they) were largely the result of the hostility of President Jackson to the Bank of the United States. . . . Millions of acres of government wild lands were bought for purely speculative purposes. Unfortunately . . . industry, and consequently production, declined, and in 1836 many articles of prime importance com-

STATE OF GEORGIA

5

The

BANK OF MORGAN

FIVE DOLLARS

105 | Many notes of the 1850s could be considered master works of engraving.

manded exorbitant prices." Jackson attempted to stem the tide of speculation through his "specie circular" of 1836 which made it mandatory to pay for government lands in gold or silver. But this only exacerbated matters, for soon the banks ran out of specie. On May 10, 1837, the storm broke. New York banks were compelled to suspend specie payments, then banks there and in other parts of the country began falling "like leaves of the Vallambrosa tree."

To relieve the shortage of "hard cash" many communities and private individuals resorted to printing their own money. These were the notorious "shinplasters," fractional notes below one dollar. A newspaper in Iowa decried the influx of shinplasters, lamenting, "As for the poor—God help them." A report from the South tells of a man who decided to make a trip and "packed his wallet with all sorts of shinplasters he considered

most likely to be accepted. His first night at the tavern . . . he asked the tavern keeper to look through the wallet and select the notes most acceptable. The keeper reportedly looked through the shinplasters, and told the traveler there was nothing in them of value, and bade him go in peace."

The country eventually rallied and by 1842 was rolling along on a new wave of prosperity. The banking business boomed along with business in general. After being introduced in 1838 in New York, the "Free Banking Act" spread to many states. This act authorized any person to procure a charter and engage in the banking business if he complied with certain conditions without obtaining a special legislative act. Banking was changed from a monopolistic privilege to a business open to all. The provisions of the act required banks to pledge securities with the supervisory authorities

against their circulating notes. Reflecting the popular reaction against the privileged character of special charters and the desire for more opportunity to invest in bank stock, "free banking" varied from state to state. It contributed to a proliferation of weak banks. "Many of these free banks came into existence," writes McCulloch, "with no more actual cash capital than was required to cover the engraver's bills, and to pay for the scanty furniture of rented banking rooms."

In 1836 the Independent Treasury System was authorized and subtreasuries were set up throughout the country in order to decentralize the Treasury's transactions with the public, for it was in this year that the Bank of the United States ceased to function as fiscal agent of the Treasury. With this arrangement, all government funds would be kept in government vaults rather than in banks.

107 / In those times of uncertainty banks tried to stress the safety factor.

Because the physical transfers of cash were both inconvenient and expensive, the use of banks was resumed. But the Independent Treasury System was maintained until 1920 when the twelve Federal Reserve Banks took over the functions of the subtreasuries.

Although the term "wild-cat" banking has become part of our tradition, it unjustly casts a shadow over the thousands of honest bankers who truly characterized the banking profession in the 19th century. Nevertheless, it was the few swindlers and speculators who attracted the most public attention, and who stirred up all the caustic wit of journalists and cartoonists. And it is a fact that speculators did establish banks and issue notes in places far away from civilization, "out among the wild cats," where nobody could reach them to redeem the notes. "I visited one of those banks once," a contemporary

wrote. "It was in a logging camp in the thick woods . . . . It was about eight feet square . . . made of rough boards, with . . . a plain shelf on which the notes were signed, a small door, over which, in red chalk, was the name of the bank. It was never occupied but once." In the aftermath of failure, the assets of another bank were found to consist of "thirteen sacks of flour, one iron safe, a counter, desk, stove-drum, and three arm-chairs."

A Midwestern bank examiner once asked to see a bank's assets and was shown some loose gold and silver coins in the drawer and nine sealed boxes. When the boxes were opened, only one was actually full of silver coins; the remainder were filled with nails and broken window-glass covered with a thin layer of coin. No wonder the public branded bank notes with such disdainful names as "stumptail," "brindle-pup," "red-

108 / John Thompson (1802-91), a New York banker well-known for his counterfeit detectors.

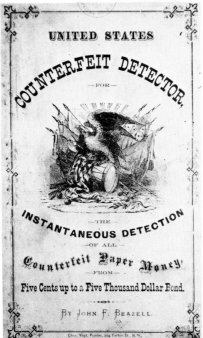

109 / There were many counterfeit detectors and listings of counterfeit and worthless notes; even listings of signatures were published for comparison purposes.

horse." Canal workers in Indiana in 1843 had similar colorful names for scrip: "white dogs" were a state issue to pay for canal repairs; "blue dogs" were receivable for canal tolls; "blue pups" were shinplasters issued by the canal contractors. In Ohio, the nomenclature was even wilder: "yellow dog," "red cat," "smooth monkey," and "sick Indian."

In some states reactions to the proliferation of worthless paper money were drastic. In 1846 Iowa decreed that "No corporate body shall hereafter be created, . . . with the privilege of making, issuing, or putting in circulation any bill, check, ticket, certificate, promissory note or other paper, or the paper of any bank, to circulate as money." By 1852, there were nine states in which banking was actually illegal!

But "hard times" were easily forgotten, and when the sun of prosperity shone brightly people continued to invest. At midcentury the great attraction was railroads. Few were aware of the recurrence of twenty year business cycles: 1818 had been a year of recession, so was 1837, and so too would it be in 1857. Ominous signs of crisis quickly gave way to panic when the New York branch of the *Ohio Life Insurance and Trust Company* had to suspend operation in August 1857. Interest rates rose sharply, and then other banks closed "as tenpins knock one another down." Mid-October found Wall Street in a frenzy: "Check after check was presented and paid, and still they came . . . until the whole lower part of the city was alive with excitement." On October 13, with thirty to forty thousand persons milling around on Wall Street, the decision was made in New York to close. Banks throughout the South and Southwest soon followed suit.

Recovery was slow this time, for

110 / Some of the leading financiers of the day, such as (from left to right) Russell Sage, Augustus Belmont, Jacob Little, and Cornelius Vanderbilt, are seen mingling with the crowds on Wall Street during the panic of October 1857.

the monetary situation was more confusing than ever. About seven thousand different kinds of valid notes were circulating—to say nothing of more than 5500 varieties of fraudulent ones. By 1862, only 253 banks issued notes which had not somehow been altered or imitated. "No holder of bank bills knew from one day to the next how much he was worth." Bills quoted as bankable one day were thrown out the next, and daily bulletins on the validity of notes became indispensable.

For the safety of the public, a Wall Street banker named John Thompson began issuing a *Bank Note and Commercial Reporter,* with facsimile signatures of the president and cashier of nearly every bank. Many counterfeit lists were published, in Cincinnati even one in German. The press tried to keep current on bank failures and on spurious notes. Banks kept their bills in drawers with four to five compartments. The first was for notes from stable eastern banks with a rating "good as gold;" the next two were for "bankable funds," from Virginia, Maryland, Kentucky, Ohio, Indiana, Illinois, and Wisconsin; while the last compartment was labeled "Western Mixed." That one, the vigilant banker watched closely, and if it began to fill up it caused him "much anxious concern."

Design and Manufacture of Bank Notes

"No Other Country Has Yet Anything to Compare With Them"

Since issuing notes was one of the primary functions of banks during the first half of the 19th century, an essential problem facing them was protection against counterfeiting. The *Bank Note Reporter* of the 1860s advised its readers to "Refuse the notes of all banks not found here." In general the number of "dangerous" counterfeits was relatively small, and experts could detect nine out of ten immediately. The main reason for this was the care most banks devoted to the manufacture of notes. Time was, when banks did their own printing in the basement, but specialized firms had long since taken over, firms with security systems which could have competed with that of Fort Knox today.

In 1862, a very observant reporter from *Harper's Magazine* toured the Wall Street headquarters of the *American Bank Note Company,* then the nation's leading firm. His remarks and the

accompanying sketches provide an excellent backstage view of "money making." The first thing that struck him was the tight security: "A man may have been for years employed in one department without ever having visited the others," he remarked. Next, he marvelled at the quality of the notes: "No other country has yet anything to compare with them." It was a fact that the very best talent was engaged to produce notes which remained unsurpassed in the beauty of their engraving and the painstaking care given to technical perfection. Sometimes the engraving of one single "vignette" — the little image or portrait adorning a note—took four months! Vignettes were the handiwork of specialized artists employed for their unique skills with portraits, or landscapes, or some other design element.

Specialization was in fact the guiding principle. From the pictorial engraving room where the drawings were cut into metal, the reporter moved into the lathe room with its specialized machinery. There, very skillful workers turned out the extremely intricate design of rosettes, called "checks" and "counters," which surrounded the large numerals on notes. The idea was to render counterfeiting impossible, since these lines were of a "delicacy and precision altogether unattainable by the human eye or hand." Inside the machine-made rosettes, other artisans hand-engraved the numerals and letters.

The next stop was at the transfer room where the engraved dies were transposed by means of powerful presses and through the intermediary of rollers, to plates used in the actual printing of the notes.

Workers in the modeling department selected and arranged designs for customers. The same

111 / During the panic in front of the Seamen's Savings Bank *on Wall Street, a ragpicker hesitates to "cumber his bag with such worthless trash" as a bundle of railway scrip thrown into the gutter by its irate owner.*

vignettes could be used by various banks, so long as the precise combination differed sufficiently. From portfolios of proofs bankers could make appropriate selections — according to their political affiliation, or the sort of clientele they catered to, or their location, or any other criteria. The *American Bank Note Company* kept approximately 8,000 plates in a special room under heavy guard. With these they printed notes for more than fifteen hundred banks in the United States and abroad, as well as numerous treasury bonds.

In the printing room, almost a hundred presses were kept continually operating. Each note had to go through three or four separate printings, according to its

112 / *The* Mercantile Agency *was formed in 1841 by Lewis Tappan to provide credit information. It is the forerunner of the* Dun & Bradstreet Company *which made credit ratings popular.*
Lewis Tappan (1788-1873).

color scheme. Endless research went into the composition of indestructible colored inks. The great pride of the company was in having developed a green ink which could not be altered without destroying the texture of the paper, nor could it be photographically counterfeited. We may assume that the predominance of green on bank notes and United States Treasury notes, prepared at that time by the company, was determined by this security factor.

Perhaps most amazing is that all the labyrinthine safeguards against counterfeiting did not diminish the esthetic quality of the notes. Although their kaleidoscopic profusion may have plagued our great-grandfathers, they will forever remain a monument of artistic and technical excellence. True artists, some well known but most anonymous, created in the bank notes of the first half of the 19th century a rich chronicle of that period.

113 / *Robert Dun (1826-1900).*

Gold Dust Banking

115 / *One of the first banks in San Francisco, the* Naglee and Sinton Bank, *established in January 1849.*

116 / *Colonel Henry M. Naglee stamped gold ingots with the bank's name.*

117 / *Millions of dollars worth of gold dust and nuggets were weighed on these large scales at the Mint in San Francisco.*

Bankers Followed the Path of the Miner

"The California gold fever is approaching its crisis. We are told that the new region . . . is El Dorado after all." This was the news that reached the East in 1848. An enormous wealth spilled from the western lands: about 25 million dollars in gold was mined in California in 1849, almost 49 million in 1850, and 60 million in 1851. Miners carried gold dust and nuggets in their buckskin belts or long purses, but when larger amounts accumulated they had to find safekeeping for their treasure, and often merchants were asked to provide this service. One such man was said to have improvised a vault in an excavation a yard square under his bed: "its compartments were buckskin bags, and the time-lock was a revolver of large caliber." Other merchants kept gold dust in tin pans or tin pots. These circumstances were more than propitious for the creation of banks, and it is only natural

that the banker followed the path of the miner.

One of these early bankers in California was Captain Henry M. Naglee from Philadelphia, who, in partnership with Richard Sinton, opened a bank in San Francisco on January 9, 1849. In addition to an ingot stamped with his name, Naglee also left a fine reputation. When a run on his bank forced him to close it, he remained in town until he could pay his obligations to the last penny. During the Civil War he joined the Union Army.

The Constitution of California prohibited the chartering of banks or "the issuing of bank notes of any description," but permitted the formation of associations "under general laws for the deposit of gold and silver." A specific law of April 1855 prohibited the issue of paper money. This aversion became a long-standing tradition: California later resisted even na-

tional bank notes not convertible into gold. Paper circulated at a discount of 40 percent compared to gold. In 1851, a bank proudly advertised: "Our security is the best in the world—Gold!"

All this greatly impeded normal transactions because gold dust and nuggets had constantly to be weighed and tested for purity. This resulted in some private coining of gold "tokens" or ingots bearing the banker's or assayer's name. Numerous such gold pieces, many the size and shape of United States gold coins, have perpetuated the memory of names such as Argenti, Naglee, Kohler, Moffatt, and many others.

The necessity of collecting the gold from the mining camps and shipping it "back east" for supplies, led to a type of business venture which combined shipping with banking. Among the many houses were *Page, Bacon & Company; Adams & Company*, a sub-

sidiary of the *Boston Express Company* of Alvin Adams; and the well known *Wells, Fargo & Company*. The latter was an off-shoot of an eastern outfit started in New York in 1849. It soon had almost a thousand stagecoaches on the roads to the mines, employed agents throughout the United States and abroad, and gained an international reputation.

The efficiency of companies such as *Wells, Fargo* could certainly compare favorably with many eastern banks, but Californians still felt the need for an organized banking system. A newspaper insisted in 1855 that "We need chartered banks whether with or without the paper currency: we must have corporations for banking, just as we have corporations for mercantile, mining, or mechanical purposes."

Unusual conditions generated a special breed of banker. "It was a gambling age—it was an age of

119 / *The San Francisco shipping firm of* Wells, Fargo and Co. *soon became famous, as did its banking subsidiary. The ad from a local newspaper of 1855 shows how widespread its activities were.*

75

speculation," was the recollection of an "old timer," and California banking had its share of strong and outstanding personalities. Darius Ogden Mills (1825-1910), a cashier from a Buffalo bank, opened the first bank in Sacramento in 1849 and then became the co-founder and first president of the *Bank of California.* William C. Ralston (1826-75), who came to California to go into steamboating, became one of the state's leading bankers. It is said that "Ralston had a marvelous head for business . . . But he had an odd supplement to the cold boiled faculty of money making, a sort of richly oriental imagination that looked far beyond the mere acquisition of a pile of cash." In 1864 Ralston and Mills founded the *Bank of California.* After Mills retired as president, Ralston carried the bank into many grandiose enterprises, "some of them sound and profitable," as one author says, "others fas-

120 / *William C. Ralston (1826-75), the founder of the* Bank of California, *was deeply involved in gold transactions.*

121 / *William Sharon (1821-85) was Ralston's agent in organizing banking operations in the Comstock region of Nevada.*

cinating but highly speculative." After the rich mines of the Comstock Lode in Nevada began producing, Ralston opened agencies in Virginia City and Gold Hill. But a run on his bank in 1875 was more than he could take, and a heart attack, or a swimming accident (or suicide) ended his life on the same day his bank closed. "Mr. Ralston went down like a giant sequoia," remembered a friend.

Banking played an important role in the other gold-producing areas such as Montana, Nevada, and Colorado. Even if the life of a banker was something less than glamorous in many of those places, his function remained the same. Primarily, he helped channel wealth eastward. In 1865, a banker

in Virginia City summed it up: "I'm still running it all alone, being president, cashier, and clerk all in one . . . We sometimes carry more gold dust in the safe than 2 or 3 men can carry . . . We sell one man currency, . . . the next a draft, the next gold dust and the next gold coin, the next a foreign draft on London, Dublin, or Germany

and perhaps the very same day buy back drafts, gold, dust, and currency."

The brothers Milton E. and Austin M. Clark, associates with E. H. Gruber, operated a bank and mint in Denver, Colorado, in the 1860s, "to refine all obtainable gold and run it into slugs and bars of convenient size, with their rela-

122 / *The modest exterior of this bank in Virginia City, Montana, in 1866, is highly misleading. Its president stated that "sometimes we carry more gold dust in the safe than two or three men can carry."*

Shipment of Treasure.

The steamers Columbia and Cortes yesterday carried away on freight the sum of $1,755,488 in gold dust. This is $89,944 less than was forwarded on the 16th ultimo, on which occasion the amount sent was $1,845,432. The shipments on the 1st of February of last year amounted to $2,430,035.

BY THE COLUMBIA, VIA PANAMA.

Page, Bacon & Co	$391,000	Hellman Bros & Co	$8,600
Burgoyne & Co	150,000	Daniel Gibb & Co	7,500
B. Davidson	115,200	Spatz & Newhouse	6,450
Wells, Fargo & Co	53,296	Gronfrier, Jan. & Co	3,600
Case, Heiser & Co	28,814	A. Cohen	1,600
F. Argenti & Co	23,928		
Total			$789,988

BY THE CORTES, VIA NICARAGUA.

Page, Bacon & Co	$420,000	Wyckoff & Co	$8,000
Adams & Co	300,000	J. H. Spring	2,000
Drexel, Sather & Chu.	75,000	Wm Steinhart & Co	6,800
C K. Garrison	52,400	Clark Rogers	5,730
Wells, Fargo & Co	55,545	J. R. Miller	5,185
J. Seligman & Co	11,000	H. Travers	5,240
Ulmer & Feissnham	18,600		
Total			$965,500

tive values stamped on them." A reporter described their $10 pieces as "exceedingly neat and tasty," showing on the reverse a view of Pike's Peak "natural as life." Such gold "slugs" might puzzle many bankers today. Still, they should not be treated as fossils of a strange period in the history of banking, but as invaluable documents of an era when bankers had to adjust to difficult conditions and create for them and the country new resources of wealth.

Ethnic Banks—Women in Banking

125 / *The German immigration made a substantial contribution to the banking industry.*

126 / *A ten "Thaler" note from the* Northhampton Bank *in Pennsylvania, 1838, printed in German and displaying the pictures of German poets and artists.*

127 / *Bilingual note—English and French—from New Orleans, about 1860.*

124 / *A lounge for ladies in a bank, late 1800s.*
◄

Ethnic Elements in American Banking

Many immigrants brought with them their national characteristics, which found an echo in American banking practices. A group of German bankers from Northampton, Pennsylvania, decided in 1835 to issue a *Zehn Taler*—a ten-dollar—note written in German with Gothic letters. The images on the note, representing German men of letters, arts, and sciences, were an unmistakable sign of the cultural level of those immigrants. Another series of notes issued a few years later in New Orleans by a French group from the *Banque des Citoyens de la Louisiane* were printed with English and French text. The back of its ten-dollar notes carried a large *Dix*—the French word for ten—and from these notes is said to have come the nickname "Dixie"—meaning "people from the land of the dix-ies."

Although the German language note remains unique, the influence

128 / *Amedeo Pietro Giannini (1870-1949) the prominent Italo-American banker, founder of the* Bank of Italy–*today the* Bank of America, *the world's largest bank.*

THE BANK OF ITALY has been, from its inception and is now, ready and anxious to make loans to people owning, or intending to build, their own homes — to the smaller mortgage borrowers who need $1000 or less. ¶ The BANK OF ITALY has built up, its present reputation, its present enormous resources, largely through catering to the small depositor—the wage earner, the producer, the small business man, the man who owns a small home or a piece of improved property, the man who is the bone and sinew of Southern California's progress. ¶ This bank has never catered to speculators. ¶ To men of the home-owning type particularly, we hold out now the opportunity to effect a loan, the opportunity to borrow money on their small holdings. ¶ And in this bank there is no need for the payment of brokers' fees or commissions, no need for working through a third party, no expenses in connection with the drawing of mortgage papers. ¶ No cost of any kind.

of the German ethnic group on banking in the United States was considerable. Many bankers proud of their background added the word "German" to the name of their bank, indicating also that their services were oriented mainly toward their compatriots. Actually, the only ethnic banks found in the *Bankers' Almanacs* during the mid-1800s were German-American. *Bepler's Banknoten-Liste*, a counterpart to the counterfeit detectors of the period, was printed in Cincinnati in the 1860s to keep the German community abreast of monetary matters. World War I changed this picture; many bankers tried to avoid public animosity by dropping their ethnic designation, "German," or by changing the name of their bank completely.

Another ethnic element strongly represented in American banking is the Italian. Its greatest representative is Amedeo Pietro Giannini,

the founder of the *Bank of Italy*, known since 1930 as the *Bank of America* and today the world's largest bank. Giannini, who cut an unprecedented trail of success in the banking world, was proud to serve the Italian community, extending a helping hand to the man of limited means. In 1919 half of his bank's 74 million dollars on loan was in the hands of farmers, packers, and canners, who could offer as securities only farm tools, dried fruit, eggs, butter, and cattle. An ad of 1913 addressed itself to the "smaller mortgage borrowers who need $1,000 or less."

California had many other ethnic banks, including the *Nippon Bank* in Sacramento, the *Canton Bank* of San Francisco, and the *Portuguese-American Bank* in the same city. Ethnic groups often made use of their native language as a special advertising feature, and thus banking ads in Polish,

Hungarian, Swedish, Spanish, and other tongues are not rare. Americans of Czech and Slovak origin proudly advertised during the 1920s that they controlled 103 banks, with heavy concentrations in the Chicago area and in Nebraska.

The Jewish contributions to American banking have been numerous and important. They date as far back as the time of the Revolution, when a Jew born in Poland, Haym Solomon (1740-80), was given the official title of "Broker of the American Revolution" for the help he accorded to the American cause. Later, the Belmonts, Guggenheims, Schiffs, and many other Jewish bankers had brilliant and distinguished careers. But not less interesting is an episode from the Jewish section in Chicago, where banks were closed on Saturdays and open on Sundays. One banker, pressed for cash on a Sunday when he could not pro-

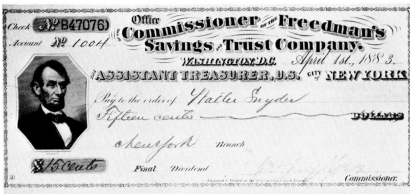

131 / The Freedman's Savings and Trust Company *chartered by Congress in 1865 eventually operated 44 branches throughout the South.*

132 / *Negro women found employment in their banks. Mrs. Agnes Reese was first bookkeeper at the Savings Bank in Richmond in the early 1900s.*

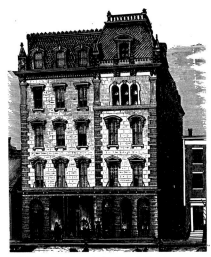

130 / *The Freedman's bank building in Washington, D. C.*

cure it from other banks, put up a sign indicating that he was making his payments in Russian rubles, of which he had a large supply. He paid out about $20,000 in rubles, thus proving his solvency, at least to his depositors familiar with Russian money.

An interesting chapter in American banking deals with the contribution of Blacks. During the Civil War special provisions were made for the safekeeping of pay belonging to Negro soldiers. In 1865, Congress chartered the *Freedman's Savings and Trust Company* on behalf of persons who had theretofore been held in slavery. From its Washington, D. C. headquarters the bank eventually managed 34 branches, mostly in the South. But real estate speculation reduced the bank to insolvency nine years later. The Comptroller of the Currency was left in charge of its liquidation. Many a poor, thrifty Black lost his savings; the books showed that, out of 72,000 deposits, 15,000 averaged five dollars, and 5,000 were for one

133 / T. Brigham Bishop, Ladies Banking House in New York, 1881.

dollar or less. The sad experience of the *Freedman's Bank* did not discourage Black people from organizing other banks. These were located in many cities in the South such as Richmond, Nashville, and Durham, as well as in New York and Chicago. Banks, mostly savings institutions, were successfully organized by and for the local Black communities.

One "minority" quickly appreciated in the banking world was women. Statistics for the *Massachusetts Bank* indicate a tenfold increase of female stockholders between 1784 and 1810, from 30 to 337. Women were the object of special consideration by bank officials who organized lavish ladies' departments where women could transact their business in a very pleasant atmosphere, isolated from the "rough world of men." Since certain bankers considered women "faithful, conscientious, careful, and honest in their commercial dealings," banks were a field in which women found employment. Slowly they even penetrated the inner-sanctum of the board room, becoming officers, junior partners, and even presidents. In 1868, a woman was elected in Huntington, Indiana, to the board of directors; in 1887 a woman became a bank president in Pulaski, New York. Since 1921 the *National Association of Banking Women* has represented women in banking, once man's exclusive domain.

In the Halls of the Stock Exchange

135 / "Commodore" Cornelius Vanderbilt (1794-1877).

137 / Russell Sage (1816-1906).

136 / Jay Cooke (1821-1905).

138 / Cyrus W. Field (1819-1892).

Financiers and Bankers on Wall Street

85

"Wall Street is not a long street, though it is felt a long way . . . It is not a handsome street . . . White marble, brown freestone, terra cotta, and substantial granite bespeak its wealth . . . It is not a wide street. Bids have been made from curb to curb." This description was published in 1864, at a time when the Civil War had brought on intensive speculation in gold. Most of the feverish buying and selling took place in the "Gold Room" of the Stock Exchange. Later gold was traded in the New York Gold Exchange until the premium on gold practically ceased in 1877.

The Stock Exchange, this busy place teeming with agitated crowds where "no voice is strong enough to out-screech that Indian hubbub of bids and offers," was

139 / In the 1850s transactions at the New York Stock Exchange were more informal than they are today, with brokers shouting their bids to clerks on the platform.

134 / The imposing interior of the New York Stock Exchange in 1885.

140 / Hetty Green (1834-1916), a colorful figure at the Exchange in the late 1800s. She was a skillful operator who succeeded in increasing her already fabulous fortune.

certainly different from the gatherings in the Tontine Coffee House at 40 Wall Street. Here, around the turn of the 19th century, a small group met in a rented room that the proprietor barely heated on cold winter days. Then as later in 1817 when the New York Stock and Exchange Board was constituted, and the Exchange had moved to larger quarters, this group was a close fraternity decidedly shy about any publicity. This secrecy precipitated the formation of an "Open Board of Brokers," and it is said that sometimes beams were cut away and bricks cut out to facilitate spying. It all ended in a very amiable way after the two groups were consolidated. Moreover, technical progress helped undermine secrecy; the telegraph and later the telephone opened a new era of communication which drastically changed working habits at the Exchange. In 1867, a ticker designed to carry stock quotations was installed to convey market news from the floor to the offices of various brokers. The Atlantic Cable greatly facilitated communication with Europe and some investment houses such as Cooke, Drexel, and Morgan intensified their international connections by establishing branches in foreign cities.

International firms were part of the elite at the Stock Exchange, but there were many brokers who led a rather precarious existence. In the special jargon of Wall Street, "scalpers" bought and sold in the hope of making a one-eighth per cent profit, while "guerrillas" dealt in inactive stock. Indeed, people at the Exchange had a vocabulary of their own, a language that was "pithy, pungent, scintillating, and sometimes rank." "To fly kites" meant to expand one's credit beyond judicious bounds; to "milk the street" meant to manipulate stock so cleverly as to affect prices; "a swimming market" meant everything was on the rise; a "gosling" or a "lame duck" was a broker who could not meet his obligations; a "dead duck" was bankrupt. A "curb-stone broker" got little respect, for he was a "gutter snipe who carries his office in his hat." The same picturesque language was also used in coded messages to "Buy 500 Zulu," for example, or "Loan Hickory Toadstool."

The securities bought and sold at the New York Exchange were stocks and bonds issued by corporations, or under national, state, or municipal authority. Activity increased rapidly during the second half of the 19th century. In 1857 a day's trade of 20,000 shares seemed staggering, while by 1881 the record had topped 700,000 shares. Railroads were the hottest item on the list, while much less attention was paid to mining. In

141 / *Curbstone brokers on Broad Street in New York in 1864.*

1885 petroleum stocks were excluded from the Stock Exchange and industrial securities encountered intense prejudice—indeed, bankers refused industrials as collateral for loans well into the twentieth century.

The years between 1865 and 1873 were boom times in the victorious states of the north, and an orgy of speculation set in. The struggle for control of the Erie Railroad and the New York Central was typical, involving such names as Cornelius Vanderbilt, Jay Gould, and Daniel Drew. The panic of 1873 put a temporary halt to the boom, but new railroad construction in the West ushered in a new boom. Panics such as the "Black Friday," September 24, 1869, triggered by a frenzied speculation in gold, or the more general financial crises of 1873, 1884, 1893, and 1907, all reverberated strongly in the halls of the Stock Exchange. A report in 1884 accurately stated that: "While the Stock Exchange has legitimate and invaluable uses, it is nonetheless true that it has been and is converted into a gambling arena by the great speculative operators . . . Professional men, merchants, farmers, widows, and spinsters blinded by the glare of success, and hoping to strengthen their slender income, have adventured their savings upon the treacherous sea of Wall Street." Personal miseries are long forgotten, as are most of the villains of Wall Street. Better remembered are the enormous strides the country took in those heady years. In the words of that same report of 1884, " . . . all these stocks indicate the vital relation of the Stock Exchange to the commerce and development of the country."

142 / *Reading the "stock-ticker," an invention of Thomas Edison, first introduced in 1867.*

MONEY
MADE THE COUNTRY
GROW

145 / Iron works in New York State.

143 / Ships in the harbor of St. Louis, 1871.

146 / A Chicago meat packing house, 1878.

144 / Wheat threshing by machine, 1870s.

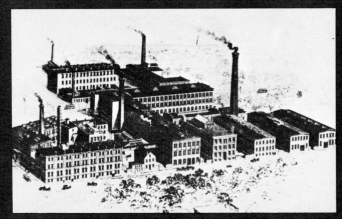

147 / Electrical plant at the Thomson-Houston
Company at Lynn, Massachusetts, c. 1890.

148 / *Train of the Central Pacific in the Sierra Nevada.*

149 / *"Forging the Shaft," 1870s.*

150 / *The East River suspension bridge, 1877.*

151 / *Work on the rapid transit in New York.*

152 / *An early automobile, 1897.*

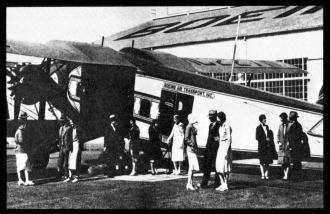

153 / *Boeing 80A in 1929.*

GREAT MEN OF FINANCE

154 / *Moses Taylor (1896-82), banker and financier of the Atlantic Cable.*

155 / *William C. Ralston (1826-75), founder of the* Bank of California.

156 / *Henry Wells (1805-78), organizer of* Wells, Fargo & Co. *and of the* American Express Company.

157 / *William G. Fargo (1818-81), his partner.*

158 / *Solomon Loeb (1829-1903), New York banker.*

159 / *Abraham Kuhn (1819-92), New York banker.*

160 / *Jacob H. Schiff (1847-1920), partner in* Kuhn & Loeb Co.

161 / *Edward H. Harriman (1848-1909), financier, railroad magnate.*

162 / *Meyer Guggenheim (1828-1905) developed mining and smelting processes.*

163 / *James Stillman (1850-1918), New York banker, helped organize the Standard Oil Corporation.*

164 / *Daniel Guggenheim (1856-1930), leading mining financier.*

165 / *John Pierpont Morgan (1837-1913), banker, formed the United States Steel Corporation, 1901.*

166 / *Andrew W. Mellon (1855-1937), banker, mining magnate.*

167 / *Amedeo Pietro Giannini (1870-1949), banker, financed early motion pictures.*

168 / Johns Hopkins (1795-1873) left his fortune to found a hospital and a university in Baltimore.

BANKERS IN THE SERVICE OF THEIR NATION

169 / George Peabody (1795-1869), founded and endowed museums in Baltimore, Cambridge, and New Haven.

170 / William Wilson Corcoran (1798-1888), philanthropist, founder of the Corcoran Art Gallery in Washington, D.C.

171 / August Belmont (1816-1890), Minister to the Netherlands, noted art connoisseur.

172 / Darius Ogden Mills (1825-1910) established hostels for the poor in New York, benefactor of the Metropolitan Museum of Art.

173 / Levi Parsons Morton (1824-1920), Minister to France, Vice-President of the United States, 1889-93.

174 / John Pierpont Morgan, Junior (1867-1943), successor to his father's firm, founded Morgan Library in New York and donated his father's art collection to the Metropolitan Museum of Art.

Banking in an Era of Industrial Expansion, 1860-1920

The Civil War Period

175 / *The imposing building of the* New York Clearing House *in 1896.*

◄

The crisis of 1857 left the country in weak condition financially. Both sides entered the Civil War with dwindling gold reserves and an unreliable paper money. In the North there was increasing distrust in the "vicious and fluctuating currency," and by 1862 the notes of all but 253 banks had been counterfeited. To Salmon P. Chase, Secretary of the Treasury, fell the formidable task of financing the war with an almost empty treasury and an alarming scarcity of hard money. Taxes met only one quarter of the government expend-

176 / *Wall Street in the fifties.*

A VISIT
TO A BANK

177 | The gentlemen of the board meet to discuss a loan application: "The question is whether Mr. Thrush's note is good enough to be discounted."

178 | Full of sense of self-importance, the newly elected cashier approaches his job a bank.

itures, the rest had to be borrowed.

In July 1861 Congress empowered Chase to issue demand notes, and in February 1862 Congress provided for the issuance of legal tender United States notes—notes which were soon nicknamed "greenbacks" because of their color on the reverse side. A group of New York, Boston, and Philadelphia bankers agreed to put into circulation 150 million dollars worth of treasury notes bearing a $7\frac{3}{10}$ percent interest. The banks pledged this amount without any profit to themselves. "So vast a responsibility, involving figures of such magnitude, had never before been attempted in this country," a contemporary remarked, comparing the sum to the assets of the Bank of England and the Bank of France combined. Chase's demand for payment in coin so depleted the supply that all banks were forced to suspend specie payments until 1879.

179 | The president of the bank receives a customer: "Let me look at your collateral note."

180 | An irate customer tries to prove to cashier that his credit is good: "Do you se Sir?"

181 | At the paying teller's window the crowd is motley: the businessman in top-hat waits in line along with a tradesman carrying a sack of coins.

182 | The runner, whose task it is to carry or to ask customers for payment, is some faced with the problem of finding his m

183 | The paper currency issued by the Confederacy depreciated rapidly, as did bank notes and numerous scrip issues.

184 | Example of scrip issued in the South by various organizations and individuals to compensate for the lack of circulating media.

Hoarding of gold and widespread speculation in securities and commodities resulted in inflation, a situation that was exacerbated by the outpouring of the government's paper currency. But the war's escalating demands for money had to be met, and Chase once vowed to keep up the effort even if it meant "we have to put out paper until it takes $1,000 to buy a breakfast." Alarmed by the public's poor reception of greenbacks, he turned to boosting bonds. In this he had the help of a young banker named Jay Cooke, who had opened a bank in Philadelphia in 1861. Cooke became the government's agent for selling public bonds, conducting a vigorous campaign using salesmen, newspaper ads, and billboards to convince the general public that their investment would be safe. He sold bonds worth 65 million dollars in 1862, 172 million in 1863, and 467 million in 1864. His bank charged only ³/₁₀ of one percent for the enormous amount of work it had to perform not only in the United States but also abroad to procure funds for the government.

A New System: The National Banks

The nationalized banking system and uniform currency sought by Alexander Hamilton and others had remained largely a utopian dream. Never was such a system more sorely missed than during the first years of the war. There were almost 1,500 state chartered banks, and in no two states was banking practice the same. In 1861 Secretary Chase proposed a national banking system to sponsor the issue of bank notes secured by a pledge of United States bonds. Chase believed that the issue of paper money by individuals or individual states infringed the rights of the Federal Government, every bit as much as the minting of coin would have.

After prolonged resistance from the state banks, this "Act to Provide National Currency" passed Congress and was signed by President Lincoln on February 25, 1863. It established a uniform national currency based upon the public credit. Its leading proponent, Senator John Sherman of Ohio, emphasized that, while these notes were not convertible, they were safe and "of uniform value." Under this law any group of five persons could obtain a national bank charter by depositing with the Treasury United States bonds worth a certain proportion of the necessary capital. They were then permitted to issue the uniform national currency.

One of the bankers who had opposed the new national banking system was Hugh McCulloch, president of the State Bank of Indiana. Through a strange turn of

Office of JAY COOKE,

Subscription Agent,

At Jay Cooke & Co. Bankers,

114 South Third Street,

Philadelphia, Nov. 1, 1862.

The undersigned, having been appointed SUBSCRIPTION AGENT by the SECRETARY OF THE TREASURY, is now prepared to furnish, at once, the

NEW TWENTY YEAR 6 PER CENT. BONDS

of the UNITED STATES, designated as "FIVE-TWENTIES," redeemable at the pleasure of the Government, after five years, and authorized by Act of Congress approved Feb. 25, 1862.

The **COUPON BONDS** are issued in sums of

$50, $100, $500, and $1000,

The **REGISTERED BONDS** in sums of

$50, $100, $500, $1000, and $5000.

Interest will commence from the **DATE OF SUBSCRIPTION**, and is **PAYABLE IN GOLD**, at the Mint, or any Sub-Treasury or Depository of the United States, on the first days of May and November of each year. At the present **PREMIUM ON GOLD**, these Bonds yield about EIGHT per cent. per annum. The ample provision made by Customs Duties, Excise Stamps and Internal Revenue, for the payment of Interest and liquidation of the Principal, makes an investment in this Loan safe, profitable and available at all times. In a word, this being the permanent Loan into which the Legal Tender Notes are convertible, it will become the PRINCIPAL LOAN in the market, and a profitable mode of investment for Trust Funds, the surplus funds of capitalists, as well as the earnings of the industrial classes.

Subscriptions received at PAR in Legal Tender Notes, or notes and checks of banks at par in Philadelphia. Subscribers by mail will receive prompt attention, and every facility and explanation will be afforded on application at this office.

A full supply of BONDS will be kept on hand for immediate delivery

JAY COOKE & CO.,

BANKERS,

FIFTEENTH STREET, Opposite the Treasury,

WASHINGTON, D. C.

Buy and Sell at current market rates, and keep constantly on hand a full supply of

GOVERNMENT BONDS,

SEVEN-THIRTIES, AND COMPOUND INTEREST NOTES.

Orders for STOCKS, BONDS, &c., executed; and Collections made on all accessible points.

186 | Jay Cooke (1821-1905), a leading banker in Philadelphia, "the clearest American mind on financial questions."

Office von Jay Cooke,

Subscriptions Agent

bei Jay Cooke & Co. Bankiers,

No. 114 Süd Dritte Straße,

Philadelphia, den 1. Nov. 1862.

Der Unterzeichnete, von dem Schatzamts-Sekretär als Subscriptions Agent ernannt, ist jetzt bereit ohne Verzug die

Neuen Zwanzig Jahr 6 prozentigen Bonds

der Vereinigten Staaten auszugeben, die als die „Fünf-Zwanziger" bezeichnet werden, indem sie nach dem Gefallen der Regierung nach fünf Jahren eingelöst werden können. Die Anleihe ist autorisiert durch einen Akt des Congreß, der am 25ten Februar 1862 unterzeichnet wurde.

Die **Coupon Bonds** werden ausgegeben in Summen von

$50, $100, $500, und $1000.

Die **Registrirten Bonds** in Summen von

$50, $100, $500, $1000 und 5000.

Die Interessen beginnen vom Tage der Subscription und sind zahlbar in Gold in der Münze, oder irgend einem Unter-Schatzamt oder Depositorium der Vereinigten Staaten, am ersten Tage des Mai oder November jeden Jahres. Zu der gegenwärtigen Gold-Prämie geben diese Bonds acht Prozent per Jahr. Die ausreichenden Vorkehrungen, welche durch Zölle, Stempelgesetze und innere Revenuen getroffen sind für Zahlung der Zinsen und Amortisation des Capitals, machen eine Capitalanlage in dieser Anleihe sicher, und vorteilhaft, und dieselbe kann zu jeder Zeit leicht realisirt werden. Mit einem Wort, da dieses die permanente Anleihe ist, in welche die „Legal Tender" Noten convertirt werden können, so wird es bald die Hauptanleihe im Markte sein, die eine vortheilhafte Gelegenheit darbietet "Trust Funds", unbeschäftigtes Vermögen von Capitalisten, und die Ersparnisse der industriellen Classen anzulegen.

Subscriptionen werden angenommen zum Nennwerth in „Legal Tender" Noten, oder Noten und Checks von Banken die "pari" stehen in Philadelphia. Subscriptionen per Post werden pünktlich besorgt und Alle die sich an diese Office wenden, erhalten jede gewünschte Auskunft.

Ein Vorrath von Bonds wird stets an Hand gehalten zur sofortigen Ablieferung.

Jay Cooke,

185 | Cooke was to sell the new bonds dubbed "5-20s". Through a very skillful sales campaign abroad, using such media as this ad in German, Cooke brought in millions for his government.

187 | The banking house of Jay Cooke on South Third Street in Philadelphia.

fate McCulloch became one of the most important protagonists of the system, for it was he whom Chase selected to become the first Comptroller of the Currency. It was the comptroller's duty to supervise the newly chartered banks, especially their lending operations. McCulloch introduced many changes, and eventually rewrote the national legislation which became the *National Bank Act* of 1864.

But state banks continued to enjoy the note issue privilege until 1865, weakening the incentive to convert from state charter to national charter. In March 1865 Congress levied a tax of 10 percent on the circulating notes of state banks. The act was revised in July 1866, and state banks found it unprofitable to continue to issue their own notes when they could convert to national charter and issue untaxed national bank notes.

In recognition for its services, Jay Cooke's bank had received

188 | *In response to the government's appeal, people exchanged gold for bonds at the Assay Office in New York in 1861.*

189 | *The new "5-20" six percent bonds matured in twenty years but could be redeemed after five years.*

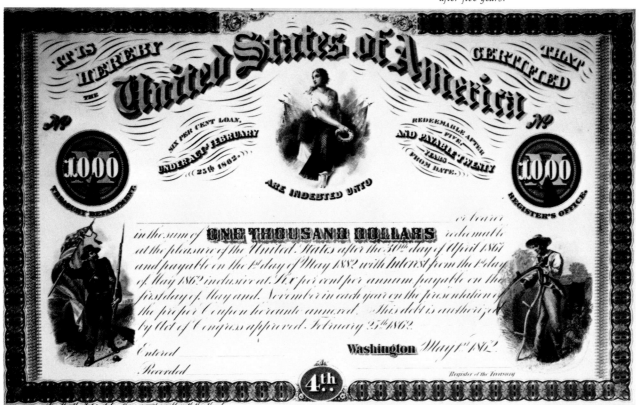

charter number one, becoming the *First National Bank of Philadelphia.* But otherwise banks had been slow in joining, one reason being their reluctance to cast off their traditional names and become simply "a number." This was changed by the 1864 law. By 1864 only 453 banks had national charters, but thenceforth the total increased rapidly, reaching the 1,500 mark within two years. The word "national" actually strengthened their credit and reputation. The system thus established destroyed the colorful multiformity of bank bills, but conferred upon the country the blessings of a uniform and trustworthy currency.

It is interesting to note that President Lincoln, who signed one of the most important of all laws regulating the country's currency and banking, was convinced that he "never had any money sense." That admission was not altogether wrong, as was shown by the hap-

hazard way he handled his personal finances, overdrawing his bank account at least twice—once because he deposited his presidential pay check five months late! His bank in Washington, *Riggs and Company,* the precursor of *Riggs National Bank,* handled the situation with understanding and tact. Some of the checks President Lincoln signed were marvelously vague, a few becoming legendary. These were made out to "Colored Man, with one Leg," or to "Mr. Johns, a Sick Man," or to "Tad (when he is well enough to present)." It is hard to imagine that a similar idiosyncracy—even in the President of the United States—would be acceptable today, which only proves that with the increase in efficiency some of the sense of humanity has been lost along the road.

190 / Salmon P. Chase (1808-73), Secretary of the Treasury, led the effort to establish a system of national banks and uniform paper currency.

191 / The National Bank Act, signed by President Lincoln on June 3, 1864.

192 / *Hugh McCulloch (1808-95), a banker from Indiana who was appointed the first Comptroller of the Currency, 1863-65.*

193 / *The first charter awarded under the National Bank Act, to the Jay Cooke bank, the First National Bank of Philadelphia, June 20, 1864.*

Banks of Wall Street— Banks of Main Streets

The reminiscences of an "old time banker," as told to a writer for the *Saturday Evening Post* in 1932, include an excellent description of banks and banking customs during the second half of the 19th century. He describes a "small bank" on lower Wall Street where he used to go as an errand boy for another banker: ". . . the bank occupied a single large room, and the president and the cashier had their desks so arranged that they saw everyone who went in or out of the bank. . . . A bank's customers were entitled, by custom, to have a look at the bank officers, and also the officers were expected to keep an eye on the clerks. . . . The banking custom of having all the officers in sight still holds in most parts of the country [in the 1930s!] . . . I have spent all my life working in full public view."

The old-timer continued: "The specie clerk was the one person in the bank whom I profoundly respected. . . . I felt somehow that he was really the bank. For if the man who had charge of the gold and silver was not the bank then who was? . . . I used to try to be in the bank on discount days—that is, when the board of directors was meeting to decide which of the notes offered would be accepted for discount. It was great fun . . . to

194 / *The new banking legislation created the office of Comptroller of the Currency within the Treasury Department.*

BANK
ARCHITECTURE

195 / *Sumptuous marble buildings, often copied from Greek temples, lined Wall Street and its counterparts in other major cities.*

196 / *Chicago's* Marine Bank.

197 / *J. P. Morgan's famous "Corner" on Wall at Broad Street, New York.*

198 / *Banking House of* Drexel, Sather and Church *in San Francisco, 1850s.*

199 / *The* Bank of California *in San Francisco.*

200 / National City Bank *of New York, one of the largest banks in the United States.*

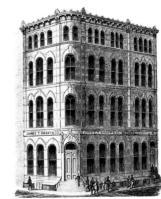

201 / *The private bank of* James T. Brady & Co. *in Pittsburgh.*

202 / Lavish interiors, adorned with crystal chandeliers, marble columns, and palms, were the pride of many banks.

watch the anxious men standing about. Some of them kept very quietly by themselves, tapping or shifting nervously. Others tried to pretend to be unworried by big talk about their money and their transactions. . . . Much later, I learned that the discounts that the men received were in inverse ratio to the noise they made."

There are many drawings and photographs preserving the memory of the plush beauty of marble-clad bank interiors, but the thousands of more modestly appointed medium-sized or small banks seldom inspired descriptions of their simple but efficient decor. "The bank," as our old-timer described his own small bank on Wall Street, "was not elaborate but it was substantial. Only the president and the cashier had desks and chairs. All the other desks were of the high, bookkeeping style, and, although all the clerks had stools, most of them stood all day. . . . Of

course, we did all our bookkeeping and wrote all our letters by hand. For there were no typewriters [typewriters started to come into use in the 1870s]. The account books, too, were works of art. I can today tell how far a banker's training goes by the character of his handwriting. The old banks could not tolerate sloppy penmanship."

About the functions of his bank, the old-timer went on in a slightly self-righteous tone: "Ours was a bank. We received deposits, paid checks, discounted negotiable paper and made loans on collateral. We did not sell securities, administer trust estates or mind babies. . . . A checking account was considered a privilege reserved for those who had money, and an account in our bank implied a certain standing. A new account was not opened unless the prospective depositor had a proper introduction."

Regarding checks, he wrote: "A bank check was not then the com-

mon medium of exchange that it is now, and a depositor who insisted on drawing a great number of checks for small amounts would be reprimanded by the cashier. . . . If a depositor wanted his money on a check at once, he took it to a banker, who might or might not buy it at a discount. . . . The phrases 'payable in current bankable funds' and 'payable in gold of the present standard of weight and fineness' . . . used to mean a great deal, for unless one wrote in these conditions, one was very likely to get paid in money that was worth only a fraction of its face value."

About the currency he had only a few words to say: "It was the same with the bank notes. We would take for deposit at par only the bank notes of the members of the New York Clearing House. Other bank notes we would take for collection or not at all. . . . The bankers dealt in greenbacks and uncurrent money [the notes issued

203 | *Even as the first settlers staked their land claims in Guthrie, Oklahoma, a bank was started in the open field, May 1889.*

204 | *"Funds Protected, Hall's Safe Time Lock" was an inducement of the* Merchants' Bank *of Guthrie.*

205 | *Banks housed in simple wooden structures were a frequent sight on the main streets of small towns.*

by state banks]. The period following the Civil War was a good one for the money changer and for no one else. The Federal Government had, during the war, issued currency notes called greenbacks, . . . and the value of the greenbacks depended entirely on how much faith the holder had in the United States getting on its financial feet."

The old-timer regretted that "the politicians in Congress had so many wild ideas about money that they had not provided any medium of exchange." Reading his words, we get the impression that he and other "small" bankers were proud of activities they considered legitimate banking, while they had only disdain for such things as selling securities. Yet, American banking in his day presented a kaleidoscopic view indeed. The daily routine of the old-timer was as different from that of other bankers such as the Browns, the Peabodys, and the Belmonts, as

the contrast between the architecture of their bank buildings.

"Wall Street" banking versus "Main Street" banking suggests figuratively this difference between the sophisticated and financially powerful banks on Wall Street—although we have seen that there were also modest banks on Wall Street—and the less pretentious banks that could be found in every little town in the country. As for Wall Street, another writer has left us a very colorful picture of the way it was before the Civil War: "On either side of the street is an illustrious row of banks and insurance offices, with foreign insurance agents, land agents, coal agents, railroad agents, steamship agents, and many other sorts of agents. . . . The basements swarm with brokers. . . . Add to this picture innumerable groups of earnest talking, scolding, chaffing, gesticulating men, dividing the rapid current of merchants, brokers, clerks,

foreign consuls, financiers, and commercial editors, . . . and one who has never seen the notorious thoroughfare will have a tolerable graphic idea of Wall Street."

It is true that the New York banks were the cornerstone of the country's financial structure. In 1897 fifteen New York banks and trust companies controlled four times the assets of all other national banks. The wealth of the leading banks found its expression in the lavishness of their buildings, often patterned on ancient Greek temples. Elegance of detail and interiors of polished marble were not only a symbol of power but also of dignity and respectability. The pseudo-religious character of bank buildings was sometimes seen as a manifestation of the esoteric character that certain bankers tried to confer on their profession. Yet, banking also took place in humble wood-frame buildings in western towns. The

contrast between Wall Street and Main Street was great, but both sorts of banks were crucial to the growth of the nation.

How essential banks were in the west is suggested by the situation in Oklahoma. Even as the very first settlers were moving on to newly opened land in May 1889, a big sign appeared in an open field reading *Bank of Guthrie*. That bank was ready to do business from a wagon. In the same place twenty-two days later, the *Merchant's Bank* tried to attract customers by advertising the security features of its vault. and time-lock—which was very secure indeed compared to the padlocks and iron safes of the 1850s.

Modest appearances were often misleading. For its advertising value, many California banks, or branches of eastern banks operating in California, established ties with foreign banks and financiers. English, French, German, and

207 / The check constituted a form of payment used mostly by the wealthy and especially by business people.

208 / In the early 1800s banks settled their accounts by sending a runner with a pocketfull of checks or sacks of money. Small accidents were always possible.

104

Dutch capital was constantly flowing into the country and houses like the Rothschilds and the English firm of the *Baring Brothers and Company* had representatives in the United States. After founding his firm in 1854, George Peabody of Massachusetts sent Junius Spencer Morgan, formerly a dry goods merchant in Boston, as his representative to London. Foreign investors held stocks and bonds of many corporations, mining companies, canals, banks, and railroads.

As the bank business grew it encountered difficult problems regarding the wise use of its credit. Since the early 19th century agents of wholesale merchant houses had been touring the country in search of credit information. In time, they began organizing specialized agencies to share this information with others. In 1841 Lewis Tappan, a dry goods dealer in New York, organized the *Mercantile Agency*, which became the *Dun & Bradstreet*

Company (named after two partners who later joined the firm).

The Clearing House

A great step forward was achieved through the establishment of the clearing house system which facilitated transactions between banks. That process was enormously complicated before this ingenious system was created in New York in 1853. Banks settled their accounts each Friday morning by sending around messengers, called porters, with drafts, entry books, and sacks of money, mostly gold and silver. It must have been quite a sight when sixty porters were busily running from bank to bank, bumping into each other, and blocking one another's way in great excitement and confusion. Many bad words were uttered and many errors made. As their predecessors had done a hundred years before in London, when they took a

break at a coffee house they got ready to settle accounts among themselves. They also began to have their own exchange on the steps of one of the Wall Street banks. This led to the organization of a "clearing house," later defined as "a place where all the representatives of the banks in a given city meet, and, under the supervision of a competent officer . . . settle their accounts with each other and make or receive payment of balances and so 'clear' the transactions of the day."

Each bank would send a settling clerk and a specie clerk, carrying the money to a determined location on Wall Street—later a special magnificent building in Renaissance style. The settling clerks would sit inside an oval counter while the specie clerks would make the rounds on the outside of the counter. Payments and receipts were exchanged in a rapid but orderly manner. Millions and later

209 | In times of financial crisis, special clearing house certificates of large denominations were issued to banks. Other certificates of small denominations circulated as money.

billions were thus transferred without confusion and without loss. By 1929, a weekly exchange at the New York Clearing House amounted to over nine billion dollars.

The great success attained by the New York organization led to the establishment of similar institutions in other cities: Boston (1856), Philadelphia (1858), Chicago (1865), San Francisco (1876). By 1912 there were 242 clearing houses throughout the country and their number was still growing steadily. In times of financial panic, when the country was crippled by a lack of circulating currency due to the failure or closing of banks, clearing house certificates helped provide the necessary exchange medium.

210 | At the clearing house it took specie clerks six minutes to make the round of the table where settling clerks were seated. The boxes the clerks are carrying were for checks and other papers.

211 / People seized by panic on Wall Street.

The American Bankers Association

On a cold January day in 1875, two St. Louis bankers, James T. Howenstein and Edward C. Breck, were walking home and observed a sign announcing, "Women's Suffrage Mass Meeting." Howenstein remarked, "If women can get together to heal their sorrows and woes, why cannot bankers get together to shooe their sorrows?" These casual words ultimately had far-reaching consequences. Seven months later 350 bankers from 32 states and territories convened in the Town Hall at Saratoga Springs, New York, and elected an executive committee to elaborate plans for a permanent organization. At a second meeting in October 1876 in Philadelphia the *American Bankers' Association* was founded "In order to promote the general welfare and usefulness of banks and banking institutions." By the beginning of 1877, about 1,600 banks had joined the association and their number continued growing constantly, reaching today the 14,000 mark.

In the hundred years since its founding, the ABA has made many decisions crucial to the financial well-being of the entire nation. Its actions justify the words of praise said in 1884 by Mr. Sidney Dean, author of an early banking history: "The financial talent and experience embodied in this large association of representative bankers, the questions discussed, and the information imparted, make it in fact, though not in theory, a college of banking and finance."

Unsettled Times

The National Bank Act of 1864, which rid the country of a colorful

212 / *Exhausted tellers tried to cope with frenzied customers.*

213 / *The results were disastrous, many honest bankers failed, and with them thousands of depositors.*

214 / *Jay Cooke's bank, which had been financing the Northern Pacific Railroad, closed its doors on September 18, 1873.*

215 / *The ticker at the Stock Exchange brought only bad news.*

216 / *Mad with panic, depositors stormed banks on Wall Street which displayed "Closed" signs.*

217 / *On September 20, 1873, for the first time in its history, the Stock Exchange had to close its doors in defense against frenzied crowds.*

107

but dangerously unstable currency, next had to stand the test of an extremely active economy. It had to prove that it was responsive and elastic enough to follow the economic curves of a rapidly expanding industrial growth. Even after completion of the transcontinental railroad in 1869, enormous amounts of domestic and foreign capital continued to pour into railroad construction. Unfortunately new lines were sometimes built before there was enough traffic to guarantee sufficient income. The 1870s were heralded by an unbridled boom, but in 1872 danger signs began to appear, a declining market for manufactured goods. Investors grew cautious, and railroads began having trouble finding financial support.

The failure of the *Atlantic Bank* of New York in April 1873 signalled an approaching storm. Early in September the rumor spread that Jay Cooke's bank, considered

218 / Lines of unemployed and hungry people were indicative of the sad consequences of the panic.

a veritable Gibraltar, was in trouble due to Cooke's deep involvement with the shaky Northern Pacific Railroad. On September 18, during a run on the New York branch of Cooke's bank, his deputy decided to close the doors. This was a fatal mistake which Cooke personally would never have made, for his and the bank's assets were still strong. A contemporary remembered the effect: "Wall Street in New York and Third Street [in Philadelphia] went mad with the suddenness as well as the magnitude of the shock. . . . The result was a complete panic in the stock market, a ruinous fall in speculative prices and a general rush upon the banks by depositors." A sense of doom started to spread. If Jay Cooke's bank could fail, then who was safe? Some could scarcely believe the news, and it is said that a newsboy was arrested for shouting: EXTRA—ALL ABOUT THE FAILURE OF JAY COOKE. Wall Street was the hardest hit, and even old, well-established banks fell victim to a frenzied panic.

Harper's Magazine captured fascinating scenes of wild panic on Wall Street, with frenzied people milling around in front of *Cooke, Fisk & Hatch,* or Vanderbilt's *Union Trust,* or storming the doors of the Stock Exchange which had to close down for the first time in its history. Although banks were badly hit, specie payments were only partially suspended and the clearing houses issued loan certificates to aid financial transactions. A well-informed financier thought that "The vitals of trade were destroyed by the canker worm of credit. . . . The effect of this collapse in 1873 was as disastrous as that of 1819; but owing to the greater extent and resources of the country was not of as long duration."

Among the reminiscences of an "old-timer" looms the spectre of the panics of 1873, of 1884, of 1893, and of 1907. Although financial panics played a certain purifying role in the nation's economic evolution, it is understandable that those dramatic moments were indelibly inscribed in the minds of the people who witnessed them. "I have seen men by the hundreds drunk with money," recalls an old banker, "I have seen men by the thousands crazed by fear, as in the awful panics of 1873, 1893, and 1907. So often have I seen the most solid and respected fortunes swept away, so often have I watched the cycle from shirt sleeves to shirt sleeves, that I am inclined to regard money riches as a restless visitor who seldom sits down."

Trying to find some explanation, he continued: "During every depression since, I have heard the bankers blamed for bringing on the trouble and then for continuing it. . . . Promoters, and the like organize banks or buy into estab-

DISAPPOINTED DEPOSITORS BESIEGING KNICKERBOCKER TRUST CO.'S BUILDING AFTER BANK HAD CLOSED ITS DOORS.

219 / On October 21, 1907, loss of confidence caused a run on the Knickerbocker Trust Company. The closing of this bank again set off a panic.

KNICKERBOCKER TRUST REPORTED AS READY TO ASK FOR A RECEIVER

President Higgins Appeals in Vain to Heads of Other Trust Companies. Att'y-General Jackson in Town to Consult with Bank Superintendent.

CORTELYOU ISSUES A REASSURING STATEMENT

AID TRUST CO. OF AMERICA

It Has Twelve Millions, and as Much as May Be Needed Is Pledged.

J. P. MORGAN IS TO HELP

With Other Financiers He Acts at Night Meeting with Secretary Cortelyou.

THE SITUATION CLEARING

Government Aid Pledged and Cortelyou Will Supervise for the

220 / A decisive step to curb the panic was undertaken by J. Pierpont Morgan.

lished banks. They cut big figures for a while . . . [but] at the first signs of trouble, the new bankers start heading backward more rapidly than they went forward. . . . The inevitable crash finds the old-line banker holding the bag. He is left slowly to build up again the credit . . . and silently to take the blame for all that has happened."

The ominous twenty-year cycle again cast its shadow over the economy in 1893, when another

panic occurred. The lessons of 1857 and 1873 had been soon forgotten, as speculation in securities, especially railroad securities, ran rampant and the basic tenets of sound financing were ignored. The results were disastrous. The year 1893 started with a series of railroad failures in Pennsylvania. This caused many banks to close—more than 500 by September—and the nation was plunged into hardship and tragedy. Only the failure of the St. Nicholas Bank in New York in December brought any smiles, for it seemed "rather hard for St. Nicholas to go broke the week before Christmas." This panic of 1893 was followed by a serious business recession, and recovery was much slower than before. As in 1873 clearing house certificates were issued, those for small amounts circulated as money, thus helping to alleviate the hardship caused by the shortage of currency.

Neither private speculation nor

Pay Roll Check

№ 1832

Chicago NOV 16 1907 190 7

Pay to the order of ————— BEARER ————— $1.00

One ————— ONE ————— Dollars

NOT OVER ONE DOLLAR

Payable only through Chicago Clearing House.

To **THE CONTINENTAL NATIONAL BANK OF CHICAGO.**

N. R. ALLEN'S SONS COMPANY

221 / *Payroll checks also circulated as money.*

110

the banking system itself could be entirely blamed for past tragedies. An inflexible governmental monetary policy greatly contributed to it. Reforms, though sought by many, were slow to come. The new century started with a great boom in the economy and in banking, but many banks had dangerously low reserves. On October 21, 1907, loss of confidence in the stability of certain banks in New York caused a run on the *Knickerbocker Trust Company.* The closing of this bank again set off a panic. The storm soon gathered force and engulfed not only trust organizations and banks in New York but also spread throughout the country. Suspension of cash payments had become widespread by November, and once again the clearing houses went into action. Soon, more banks were using emergency scrip than ever before. Cashier's checks and payroll checks often took the place of money.

A decisive step in curbing this panic of 1907 was undertaken by the prominent banker John Pierpont Morgan. Since this panic was dominated by a distrust among banks, Morgan rallied the support of other leading Wall Street bankers to raise a fund of 35 million dollars which could provide backing for the hard-pressed banks. The White House got closely interested in developments, and support and sympathy were extended both by President Theodore Roosevelt and his Secretary of the Treasury, George B. Cortelyou.

The panic of 1907 provided convincing evidence that, if further disasters were to be avoided, the country needed an "elastic" currency which could increase in volume when demands on banks necessitated it.

Services Rendered by Banks

In the years after 1873 the entire economy of the country started changing as a result of industrial growth. This substantial increase in the number of corporations directly affected the money market and banks. Investment bankers and brokers now started selling corporate industrial securities as well as government bonds and railroad mining stock. Some American banking houses also became prominent in foreign finance. In the east, international ties were a tradition established during the first half of the 19th century by merchant bankers such as the Brown Brothers. A worldwide network of corresponding banks using circular letters of credit opened up enormous financial resources. After the discovery of its fabulous mineral riches, the west became a focus of international attention; most of the banks in the gold regions had widespread connections. Cities such as St. Petersburg, Sidney, Yokohama, or Shang-

222 / *Banks took pride in their lavish architecture: the sumptuous building of the* Union Trust *of Philadelphia.*

hai were as much within reach as London or Paris.

The discovery of gold in California affected the money market in other ways. Gold became an important consideration in domestic as well as international trade, as is suggested by the establishment of the special "Gold Room" at the New York Stock Exchange. The suspension of specie payments during the Civil War made gold a highly desirable commodity and only its official reappearance in 1879 lowered the high premium on it. Gold, therefore, found a conspicuous place in bank advertising.

Multifaceted banking institutions satisfying numerous financial needs started to become common toward the end of the century. Savings institutions, popular because of their socially appealing character, multiplied rapidly. Institutions with names such as "Dollar Savings Bank," "Dime Bank," or even "Penny Savings Bank" were frequent sights throughout the country. Trust companies began to increase considerably in number after the turn of the century. And bankers paid more attention to the small patron. The result was that many a bank was converted into a veritable "department store of finance." They developed special departments—savings departments which kept Saturday afternoon and evening hours to suit the needs of the wage-earning class; loan departments which based transactions not only on collateral securities but also on one's general credit; and trust departments which kept an eye on one's assets and investments. Banks also organized bond departments and real estate loan departments.

Safe deposit facilities rapidly became popular. A New York banking concern sought to cater to the needs of the "New York 400," the very rich who could use the facilities of a safe box to deposit their jewels late after theater hours or enclose the bundles of their stock papers after the market closing hours. This "Night and Day Bank" which opened in 1906 on Fifth Avenue at 44th Street, extended the usual six-hour day to a full twenty-four hours, serving its clients in a plush ambience of marble and velvet. Sponsored by Edward H. Harriman, who was also one of its directors, the bank outlived its usefulness. When its rich clients moved further north on Fifth Avenue it changed its name in 1911 to the *Harriman Trust Company.*

Most of the securities, rails, and industrials, as well as many municipal bonds, were handled by investment bankers located not just in New York but also in such places as Chicago and St. Louis. Names such as Russell Sage, whose bank's motto was "Security, scrutiny, secrecy," and Edward H. Harriman, were intimately associated with the powerful but very risky

arena of railroad financing. The dawn of the monopolistic power of the trusts began to appear. The one name that has survived in the public memory as the epitome of colossal financial success and power is that of John Pierpont Morgan. He was the son of a prominent banker, Junius Spencer Morgan, an associate in the Drexel firm which occupied the famous building on Wall Street known as "the Corner." J. P. Morgan gained the reputation of undisputed leadership in the investment field. The frequent railroad bankruptcies of the 1890s gave him a strong grip on the transportation field, to which he added the famous *United States Steel Corporation* in 1901, which truly made him the "Money King."

Bank Advertising

Bank advertisements show a distinctive trend in their evolution since colonial times. They symbo-

223 / Bank ads of the mid-1800s were simple and to the point.

224 / Slogans could often prove a good eye catcher.

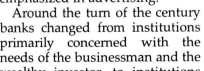

lize the relationship between the banker and his customers. Conforming to general practice, bank advertisements of the mid-1800s were sober and to the point, listing available services with simple clarity. In the second half of the 19th century, lavish architecture, the pride of many banks, was often emphasized in advertising.

Around the turn of the century banks changed from institutions primarily concerned with the needs of the businessman and the wealthy investor, to institutions

225 / Humor became a common motif.

112

POOR OLD COLUMBUS, BORN FIVE CENTURIES TOO SOON!

The Pen That Changed the Course of a Nation

226 / *Historical reminiscences proved very striking.*

227 / *The luxurious interior of the* Safe Deposit Company *in San Francisco.*

228 / *In the 1870s vaults in San Francisco were not only safe but also elegant.*

whose aim was to serve the entire population. This change is reflected in bank advertisements. Safety and reliability became a main theme of many advertisements in the early 1900s, since financial panics of the past had made bankers sensitive to how important this was to patrons. During World War I thrift was highly stressed.

In the 1920s the style became more graphic and imaginative. Ladies were given special attention. Giveaways were particularly colorful, and calendars with a lacy or flowery border, or bookmarks, were designed to please the female taste. Advertising men tended to stress new, "never before seen" elements to elicit desired psychological effects. After World War II, advertisements became even more colorful and bold, humor being a common element, while a note of nostalgia was added through historical reminiscences.

113

230 / *Nelson W. Aldrich (1841-1915), Senator from Rhode Island.*

229 / *Among the many agencies created in 1933 to pull the nation from depression, the* Federal Deposit Insurance Corporation *(FDIC) helped restore confidence in the banking system.*
◄

231 / *Carter Glass (1858-1946) of Virginia, co-author of the Federal Reserve Act.*

The Federal Reserve System

The panics of 1857, 1873, 1893, and especially 1907 revealed deep flaws in the nation's monetary system: the reserve requirements were unsatisfactory, the check collection system was cumbersome, the relationship between banks and the Treasury was tenuous, and, above all, the currency lacked elasticity when most needed. When confronted with exceptionally heavy demands, banks had no way of bolstering reserves. This shortcoming triggered frenzied runs on banks which bring to mind an episode which happened during an earlier panic when a depositor, seeing his money being paid out to him said, "I don't want it now that I have seen it."

It began to appear more and more obvious that any semblance of stability was contingent upon the reestablishment of a central-

115

232 / *Robert L. Owen (1856-1947), Senator from Oklahoma who secured passage of the Act in the Senate.*

233 / President Woodrow Wilson.

ized bank. The alarming events of 1907 underscored the necessity for Congressional action. In 1908 a *National Monetary Commission* was appointed, and in 1911 it presented a plan of reform. This was largely the work of its chairman, Nelson W. Aldrich (1841-1915), Senator from Rhode Island. The *Aldrich Plan* called for establishing a *National Reserve Association* of fifteen banks empowered to issue currency when needed. All banks willing to comply with certain requirements would be eligible to join in, though no bank was required to become a member. Aldrich's plan, reflecting the interests of business, met stiff opposition, and the election of the Democrat Woodrow Wilson in 1912 killed its chances altogether.

A compromise was found by Carter Glass (1858-1946), Con-

234 / The Federal Reserve Act, signed by President Woodrow Wilson on December 23, 1913.

Sixty-third Congress of the United States of America;

At the Second Session,

Begun and held at the City of Washington on Monday, the first day of December, one thousand nine hundred and thirteen.

AN ACT

To provide for the establishment of Federal reserve banks, to furnish an elastic currency, to afford means of rediscounting commercial paper, to establish a more effective supervision of banking in the United States, and for other purposes.

Be it enacted by the Senate and House of Representatives of the United States of America in Congress assembled, That the short title of this Act shall be the "Federal Reserve Act."

Wherever the word "bank" is used in this Act, the word shall be held to include State bank, banking association, and trust company, except where national banks or Federal reserve banks are specifically referred to.

The terms "national bank" and "national banking association" used in this Act shall be held to be synonymous and interchangeable. The term "member bank" shall be held to mean any national bank, State bank, or bank or trust company which has become a member of one of the reserve banks created by this Act. The term "board" shall be held to mean Federal Reserve Board; the term "district" shall be held to mean Federal reserve district; the term "reserve bank" shall be held to mean Federal reserve bank.

FEDERAL RESERVE DISTRICTS.

SEC. 2. As soon as practicable, the Secretary of the Treasury, the Secretary of Agriculture and the Comptroller of the Currency, acting as "The Reserve Bank Organization Committee," shall designate not less than eight nor more than twelve cities to be known as Federal reserve cities, and shall divide the continental United States, excluding Alaska, into districts, each district to contain only one of such Federal reserve cities. The determination of said organization committee shall not be subject to review except by the Federal Reserve Board when organized: *Provided,* That the districts shall be apportioned with due regard to the convenience and customary course of business and shall not necessarily be coterminous with any State or States. The districts thus

Approved 23 December, 1913.

Woodrow Wilson

gressman from Virginia and Chairman of the House Committee on Currency. Together with Professor H. Parker Willis of Columbia University, Glass worked out a system that vested central control with the government instead of with private bankers. Although it raised a storm of opposition among eastern bankers, it passed the House easily. After Robert L. Owen of Oklahoma secured its passage in the Senate by a vote of 54 to 34, it was signed by President Wilson on December 23, 1913.

The *Federal Reserve Act* of 1913 constituted the most important modification of the nation's banking system since the *National Bank Act* of 1864. The Act, which was put into operation on November 16, 1914, created a unique banking system which combined central with regional power. All national banks were required to join; other state or private banks could join too, by complying with certain requirements. The central authority was lodged in the Federal Reserve Board, composed of the Secretary of the Treasury, the Comptroller of the Currency, and five others appointed by the President for ten-year terms. The regional power was divided among Federal Reserve banks located in Boston, New York, Philadelphia, Richmond, Atlanta, St. Louis, Cleveland, Chicago, Kansas City, Minneapolis, Dallas, and San Francisco. These 12 banks, each representing a Federal Reserve district, were devised as bankers' banks; they were to be owned jointly by the banks belonging to the system, each of which was to subscribe six percent of its capital and surplus with a regional Federal Reserve bank. These regional centers were given a certain autonomy. They could make loans to member banks by rediscounting their commercial paper, and they could buy and sell government bonds. Most important, they were to issue a new currency, Federal Reserve notes. Each bank was to be governed by a nine-member board of directors representing the interests of banking, industry, commerce, agriculture, and the general public.

Since 1917, the Federal Reserve banks have cleared checks coming from banks located out of town and out of state. They also receive new currency from the Bureau of Engraving and Printing, exchanging it for worn out currency received from member banks. Furthermore, they also provide banks with coins and currency when needed, or hold their surplus. But most significant for the financial prosperity of the country is the way the Federal Reserve controls the total volume of credit by regulating the lending power of banks. By reducing the reserve requirement it raises their lending power, while in times of inflation it can raise the rediscount rate and thus

CHARTER
OF
The Federal Land Bank of Wichita
NUMBER 9
Office of The Federal Farm Loan Board

Washington, D.C., March 1st 1917.

Whereas, The Federal Land Bank of Wichita of the City of Wichita, County of Sedgwick, state of Kansas, and in the Ninth Federal Land Bank district, has filed with the Farm Loan Commissioner, its Organization certificate as required by law, and done and performed all things required by law to be done before completing its organization; NOW THEREFORE, The Federal Farm Loan Board does hereby grant this Charter to The Federal Land Bank of Wichita, and said The Federal Land Bank of Wichita is hereby authorized and empowered to do and perform all acts, and transact all business which may be legally done, performed and transacted by a Federal Land Bank, under and in accordance with the provisions of the act of Congress, approved July 17, 1916, known as The Federal Farm Loan Act, and to do all other things implied and incident thereto, within the states of Kansas, Oklahoma, Colorado and New Mexico.

In Witness Whereof, The Federal Farm Loan Board has caused this charter to be signed by its executive officer, Farm Loan Commissioner, attested by its Secretary, and has caused its seal to be hereunto affixed this first day of March 1917.

Federal Farm Loan Board

By _____
Farm Loan Commissioner

Attest:

_____ Secretary

235 / A Federal Land Bank charter.

118

tighten credit. The Federal Reserve can also affect bank reserves by buying or selling government securities in so-called "open-market operations." The long-sought elasticity of the currency is thus attained as a safeguard against the spectre of financial panics.

Banking for the Poor

Meeting the financial needs of the farmer has been a thorny problem for a long time. Farm loans grew from less than three billion dollars in 1900 to eighteen billion in 1920, much of this carried by commercial banks. Nevertheless, farmers still felt disadvantaged. Earlier, their discontent had found expression in the Granger Movement of the late 1800s, which formed its own banks. In 1916 the federal government tried to extend a helping hand by authorizing its first

236 / Immigrants at a postal savings bank.

237 | Arthur Morris (1881-1973), "father of consumer credit."

BANK TO LEND MONEY TO POOR

BATTLE AGAINST "MONEY SHARKS" PLANNED.

PLANS FOR ORGANIZATION OUTLINED AT MEETING OF COMMITTEE OF CHAMBER OF COMMERCE — CAPITAL STOCK OF CORPORATION WILL BE $50,000.

(Atlanta Constitution, March 17, 1911.)

A loan bank which will provide the salvation for the working people of Atlanta against the "money shark" system is soon to be established.

Plans for organization were outlined yesterday afternoon at the Chamber of Commerce, and the institution will be put in operation just as soon as Atlantans have bought stock sufficient for a starting capital of $50,000.

This bank will enable the working man and women to secure loans at the legal rate of interest, 8 per cent., and repay them in small amounts, furnishing this class of borrowers banking facilities not now enjoyed by them and relief from the clutches of the professional sharks who charge exorbitant interest.

REPORT OF COMMITTEE.

238 | Advertisement in Atlanta, Georgia, 1911.

STATISTICS AS TO BORROWERS AS REVEALED BY THE MORRIS PLAN COMPANY OF NEW YORK

	6-Month Period	8-Month Period
Rent	28	45
Insurance premiums	43	79
Help relatives	61	129
Vacation	......	145
Positions or occupations of borrowers		
Clerks	247	370
Post-office employees	245	397
State department and court employees	......	33
City department and court employees	177	332
New York county employees	......	26
Firemen	198	304
Policemen	144	201
U. S. employees other than post-office	95	190
Proprietors and partners	344	435
Printers' trades	108	259
Salesmen	113	179
Bookkeepers and accountants	......	101
Factory operators	......	100
Managers	......	100
Agents	......	59
Secretaries and stenographers	......	56
Foremen	......	55
Tailors	......	53
Inspectors	......	52
Machinists	......	46
Artisans	......	35
Telegraphers and dispatchers	......	33
Teachers	......	33
Doctors and dentists	......	17
Writers	......	17
Miscellaneous	239	330
Classification According to Employment		
New York City	......	920
U. S. Government	......	610
New York County	......	35
New York State	......	23
Mercantile	......	395
Manufacturing	......	354
Newspapers	......	232
Printing and publishing	......	134
Insurance	......	118
Financial	......	115
Railroads	......	114
Public utilities	......	66
Tailoring	......	54
Telegraph and telephone	......	49
Contracting and building	......	48

	6-Month Period	8-Month Period
Borrowers		
Men	2,322	3,657
Women	122	150
Average weekly income	$25.83	$25.00
Married	1,813	2,777
Single	620	1,023
Unaccounted for	9	24
Supporting children	......	2,249
Number of children	3,932	5,849
Supporting others	......	2,601
Number of others	......	2,936
Real estate owners	359	491
Reasons for borrowing		
Repay loan sharks	172	213
Repay loans on pawns and chattels	72	123
Clean up small miscellaneous debts	670	942
Illness and births	400	713
Deaths	59	107
Weddings	16	30
Begin housekeeping	15	33
Offset increased household expenses	121	192
Purchase of home	21	28
Personal expenses	......	47
Education	55	76
Begin business	35	45
Business expansion	372	506
Mortgage and interest	......	86
Taxes	74	95

farm credit system, the *Federal Land Banks.* Designed to assist tenants in buying land, this organization provided for a division of the entire country into twelve districts, each with its land bank. These banks worked in conjunction with local loan cooperatives organized

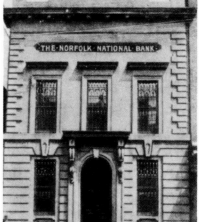

239 | Original home of the Morris Bank in Norfolk, Virginia.

240 / *Financier and philanthropist J. Pierpont Morgan, Jr., leads a Liberty Loan parade.*

241 / *Poster advertising the sale of Liberty Bonds.*

120

into the *National Farm Loan Association*. A borrower bought stock in this association equal to five percent of his loan, which could amount to fifty percent of the value of his land and twenty per cent of the value of the improvements.

In the last decades of the 19th century, savings institutions became increasingly popular. But there were no postal savings banks of the sort found in Europe. A major argument in their favor was that they would serve the needs of immigrants who had been used to such institutions in their homeland. Private banks and savings institutions naturally opposed the idea of postal savings, and ultimately made sure that such a system would offer them no serious competition. In June 1910, when Congress finally established the postal savings system, it authorized only a two percent interest on savings deposits. Nevertheless, postal savings did benefit persons

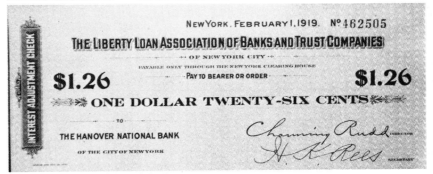

242 / *Bonds were sold through banks.*

243 / *Farmers did not share in the general prosperity.*

244 / *Many small-town banks fell victim to the bad times that hit agricultural areas especially hard.*

of very limited means who could save only small amounts.

Since banks normally loaned money to those who could put up good collateral, poor people were often left to the mercy of "loan sharks." A strong campaign against them was initiated by a Virginia lawyer, Arthur Morris (1881-1973), who established the first system of personal installment loans for wage-earners, or small business people. Morris had served as a legal advisor to several Norfolk banks, and was fully appreciative of the fact that banks could not generally afford to get involved with long-term loans for small amounts. After a lengthy study he concluded that character, plus earning power, was a proper basis for credit. In addition, he felt that loans should be repaid over a period commensurate with the earning power of the borrower and that money so borrowed should

always be for some constructive purpose.

According to the "Morris Plan" a borrower had to establish a reserve with which to pay up his loan, by saving from his weekly or monthly salary an amount that would equal his loan in one year. Morris felt that his plan encouraged both thrift and pride. Interest rates, though modest, were sufficiently profitable.

An interesting description of Morris' plan can be found in a letter he received along with his charter from the State Corporation Commissioner. The Commissioner wrote, "I have carefully considered your application for a charter for your hybrid and mongrel banking institution. Frankly, I don't know what it is. It isn't a savings bank; it isn't a state or national bank; it isn't a charity. It isn't anything I ever heard of before. Its principles seem sound, however, and its purposes admirable. But the reason

245 / The 1920s saw speculation on the stock market reach unprecedented heights.

that I am going to grant a charter is because I believe in you."

Morris managed to raise an initial capital of $20,000 and in March 1910 he opened the first "Morris Plan" bank, the *Fidelity Savings and Trust Company*, in Norfolk, Virginia, in a modest two-room office. Within three years there were twelve such banks, and by 1926 more than a hundred. The Morris plan drew the attention of the entire nation when it was announced that the *Industrial Finance Corporation*, capitalized at five million dollars, had been formed in Virginia to back institutions designed "to provide for the worthy wage earner, where the need of the loan is apparent, opportunity for borrowing small sums of money, without the necessity of submitting to the extortion of unscrupulous money-lenders, but at rates which are reasonable to the borrower and yet fairly remunerative to capital."

**WORST STOCK CRASH STEMMED BY BANKS;
12,894,650-SHARE DAY SWAMPS MARKET;
LEADERS CONFER, FIND CONDITIONS SOUND**

FINANCIERS EASE TENSION	Wall Street Optimistic After Stormy Day; Clerical Work May Force Holiday Tomorrow	LOSSES RECOVERED IN PART
Five Wall Street Bankers Hold Two Meetings at Morgan Office.	Confidence in the soundness of the stock market structure notwithstanding the upheaval of the last few days, was voiced last night by bankers and other financial leaders. Sentiment as expressed by the heads of some of the largest banking institutions and by industrial executives as well was distinctly cheerful and the feeling was general that the worst had been seen. Wall Street ended the day in an optimistic frame of mind. The opinion of brokers was unanimous that the selling had got out of hand not because of any inherent weakness in the market but because the public had become alarmed over the steady toptide.	Upward Trend Starts With 200,000-Share Order for Steel.
CALL BREAK 'TECHNICAL'		TICKERS LAG FOUR HOURS

246 / *Cartoons ridiculed the crash of the stock market in October, 1929.*

247 / *"Bread lines" became a common sight.*

123

248 | *"Change bank laws, protect savings," was the cry raised by many.*

Financing of the First World War

The outbreak of the great conflagration in 1914 marked the beginning of significant changes in the financial status of the United States. Most important, it shifted from a borrowing to a lending position in the world community. Not long before, foreign capital had played a key role in building America's railroads and industries, but during the war the United States became the world's greatest creditor. Even by 1916 Allied loans totalled nearly two billion dollars.

After the nation actually joined in the fighting in 1917, it was faced with the problem of boosting the public credit. In just two years, 1917 to 1919, the United States raised some 37 billion dollars to support the American war effort and to help the Allies. The public debt grew from less than two billion dollars to nearly 27 billion.

The banks of the nation played a decisive part in this fund-raising effort. It was reminiscent of Jay Cooke's imaginative campaign during the Civil War. Billboards and newspaper ads encouraged the purchase of government bonds, there were street-corner rallies, and prominent politicians, financiers, and actors appealed to the patriotic spirit of the people.

The Federal Reserve banks vigorously promoted the sale and redemption of certificates of indebtedness and war savings certificates. A revenue act of March 1917 authorized the Secretary of the Treasury to raise "such sum or sums as, in his judgment, may be necessary to meet public expenditures, and to issue therefor certificates of indebtedness in such form and in such denominations as he may prescribe." The rate of interest was not to exceed three percent. Beginning in June 1917 the government floated four large loans called *Liberty Loans;* a fifth, after the Armistice, in April 1919, was called *Victory Loan.* Again, the Federal Reserve banks actively promoted sales of these certificates, trying to secure the widest possible distribution among the other banks.

249 | *The government tried to lend a helping hand by creating organizations to extend credit.*

250 / "A nameless, unreasoning, unjustified terror" caused many runs on banks.

252 / Governor W. A. Comstock of Michigan proclaimed a bank holiday on February 14, 1933.

253 / Governor Herbert Lehman of New York signed a two-day holiday on March 4, 1933.

STATUS OF BANKING RESTRICTIONS BY STATES ON MARCH 4, 1933

ALABAMA—Closed until further notice.
ARIZONA—Closed until March 13.
ARKANSAS—Closed until March 7.
CALIFORNIA—Almost all closed until March 9.
COLORADO—Closed until March 8.
CONNECTICUT—Closed until March 7.
DELAWARE—Closed indefinitely.
DISTRICT OF COLUMBIA—Three banks limited to 5 per cent; nine savings banks invoke sixty days' notice.
FLORIDA—Withdrawals restricted to 5 per cent plus $10 until March 8.
GEORGIA—Mostly closed until March 7, closing optional.
IDAHO—Some closed until March 18, closing optional.
ILLINOIS—Closed until March 8, then to be opened on 5 per cent restriction basis for seven days.
INDIANA—About half restricted to 5 per cent indefinitely.
IOWA—Closed "temporarily."
KANSAS—Restricted to 5 per cent withdrawals indefinitely.
KENTUCKY—Mostly restricted to 5 per cent withdrawals until March 11.
LOUISIANA—Closing mandatory until March 7.
MAINE—Closed until March 7.
MARYLAND—Closed until March 6.
MASSACHUSETTS—Closed until March 7.
MICHIGAN—Mostly closed, others restricted to 5 per cent indefinitely; Upper Peninsula banks open.
MINNESOTA—Closed "temporarily."
MISSISSIPPI—Restricted to 5 per cent indefinitely.
MISSOURI—Closed until March 7.
MONTANA—Closed until further notice.
NEBRASKA—Closed until March 8.
NEVADA—Closed until March 8.
NEW HAMPSHIRE—Closed subject to further proclamation.
NEW JERSEY—Closed until March 7.
NEW MEXICO—Mostly closed until March 8.
NEW YORK—Closed until March 7.
NORTH CAROLINA—Some banks restricted to 5 per cent withdrawals.
NORTH DAKOTA—Closed temporarily.
OHIO—Mostly restricted to 5 per cent withdrawals indefinitely.
OKLAHOMA—All closed until March 8.
OREGON—All closed until March 7.
PENNSYLVANIA—Mostly closed until March 7, Pittsburgh banks open.
RHODE ISLAND—Closed on March 4.
SOUTH CAROLINA—Some closed, some restricted, all on own initiative.
SOUTH DAKOTA—Closed indefinitely.
TENNESSEE—A few closed, others restricted, until March 9.
TEXAS—Mostly closed, others restricted to withdrawals of $15 daily, until March 8.
UTAH—Mostly closed until March 8.
VERMONT—Closed until March 7.
VIRGINIA—All closed until March 8.
WASHINGTON—Some closed until March 7.
WEST VIRGINIA—Restricted to 5 per cent monthly withdrawals indefinitely.
WISCONSIN—Closed until March 17.
WYOMING—Withdrawals restricted to 5 per cent indefinitely.

251 / Status of banking restrictions in the states, March 4, 1933.

254 / *President Franklin D. Roosevelt.*

255 / *Headlines announce the dramatic events.*

| Section 1 | "All the News That's Fit to Print." | **The New York Times.** | LATE CITY EDITION WEATHER—Fair today and tomorrow; temperature unchanged. Temperatures Yesterday—Max. 41; Min. 34 | Section 1 |

Copyright, 1933, by The New York Times Company.

VOL. LXXXII....No. 27,434. Entered as Second-Class Matter, Postoffice, New York, N. Y. NEW YORK, SUNDAY, MARCH 5, 1933. F Including Rotogravure Picture, Magazine and Book Sections. TEN CENTS | TWELVE CENTS Beyond 200 Miles. Except in 7th and 8th Postal Zones.

ROOSEVELT INAUGURATED, ACTS TO END THE NATIONAL BANKING CRISIS QUICKLY; WILL ASK WAR-TIME POWERS IF NEEDED

CASH WITHDRAWAL LIMIT AND SCRIP BILL SPEEDED

Legislature Plans Action Today on Measure to Solve Bank Crisis; New Deposits to Be Exempt

256 / *Cartoonists point at the two main offenders: hoarders and alarmists.*

ROOSEVELT CLOSES ALL BANKS; CONGRESS MEETS THURSDAY

War-time Measure Invoked to Protect Nation's Gold; Emergency Program Awaits Special Session; Issuance of Scrip Authorized

Roosevelt Shuts Banks 4 Days,

257 / The opening of the special session of Congress on March 9, 1933, called by the President to deal with the banking crisis.

A series of eye-catching posters appeared which admonished Americans to "Beat back the Hun with Liberty Loan." There were constant reminders that the contribution of every single citizen was essential "To make the world a decent place to live in." Well-known bankers such as Jacob Schiff spoke at rallies aimed at boosting the sale of Liberty Bonds

ROOSEVELT'S MOVE DECLARED EASING ANXIETY OF PUBLIC

Secretary of Treasury Points to Banking Proclamation as Giving Him Unlimited Power to Deal with Crisis.

CONGRESS READY TO SPEED ACTION

First Move of Administration Financial Leaders Will Be Plan Permitting Unhampered Use of Checking Accounts.

A COMMUNITY BUSINESS CONDUCTED BY BARTER

Minneapolis Organized Unemployed, a Group Without Money, Operate Factory, Repair Shops, Restaurant and Store by Exchanging Their Labor for Necessities.

by explaining the reason for the Liberty Loans and their value to the individual and the nation.

The public response was astonishing. "They blew the roof off the country" was the way one reporter described the second day of selling the first Liberty Bonds. The four Liberty Loans and the Victory Loan yielded more than $21 billion; this total represented sixty-six million individual subscriptions. Secretary of the Treasury William G. McAdoo expressed a general feeling when he called the loans "a genuine triumph for democracy . . . the unmistakable expression of America's determination to carry this war for the protection of American life and the reestablishment of peace and liberty throughout the world to a swift and successful conclusion."

Years of Prosperity,
Years of Crises

The prosperity that followed re-

covery from the panic of 1907 lasted through the end of World War I. A sharp recession followed the end of the war, but recovery was quick and the "Roaring Twenties" was an era of unprecedented boom. Unfortunately, the picture was not uniformly bright; farmers, especially, did not share in the general prosperity. A collapse of agricultural prices in the early 1920s, from their high levels during and immediately after World War I, initiated a period of depressed conditions in many rural areas. This, along with the movement of population from rural to urban areas, resulted in the closing of hundreds of rural banks in the 1920s.

City people felt prosperous, however, and sales of consumer goods increased enormously. This was particularly true of automobiles and home appliances. The stock market became an interesting game to people conditioned by wartime bond campaigns. Stock

258 / Private initiative was often invaluable.

speculation increased sharply. The lending capabilities of banks were often overtaxed by loans to people who felt compelled to play the market, sometimes with little cash and much credit. The total number of shares traded grew tenfold between 1918 and 1928. Voices of reason could seldom make themselves heard, although warnings came from many competent people. In 1927 a California banker lamented

259 / *Clearing house certificates were prepared but the order was never given to release them.*

260 / *Private scrip came into circulation.*

that: "Speculation, aided by cheap money, has run riot through the country. The lessons of the past are shown but scant respect and we are told that we must adjust ourselves to modern methods and conditions, but it is our opinion that what are today called old fashioned methods, will have more respect paid to them five years from now." In fact, only two years elapsed before the virtues of "old fashioned methods" became abundantly clear. After a feverish climb, the stock market broke in October 1929 and prices immediately fell almost one-third. Bewildered crowds could not at first believe it, but the bubble had burst.

The crisis was worldwide. In Europe financial distress involved many countries. England's departure from the gold standard had grave repercussions everywhere, especially in the United States. New York, next to London the world's greatest money market,

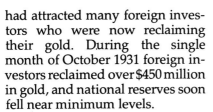

261 / Secretary of the Treasury W. H. Woodin watching the President sign the Emergency Banking Relief Act *on March 9, 1933.*

had attracted many foreign investors who were now reclaiming their gold. During the single month of October 1931 foreign investors reclaimed over $450 million in gold, and national reserves soon fell near minimum levels.

Under the impact of the general economic situation, with unemployment at a steady increase, a snowball effect of terrifying dimensions and rapidity involved the banking system. During 1930 nearly 1,200 banks failed; in October 1931 that many failed in a single month. The feeling of uncertainty which dominated the nation took alarming proportions producing disastrous results. The entire economy seemed in danger of collapsing in the face of fear. There were countless runs on banks. "No sermon on the need for confidence," one historian writes, "even if the preacher possessed the eloquence of Demosthenes and the fervor of Peter the Hermit, could

persuade a man to leave his money in a bank that he believed to be unsound. And when dozens of banks were failing every day, the sermon must have sounded sardonically hollow." Thus, the snowball effect: fear, the result of failures, became the cause of more failures.

The *Reconstruction Finance Corporation,* a two-billion dollar governmental lending agency organized by the Hoover administration in early 1932, was of limited effect in contending with a tide of hysterical panic kindled by a continued alarmistic propaganda. Improvement on the international money market helped little; neither did proposed banking reforms sponsored by Senator Carter Glass

of Virginia. The presidential election campaign of 1932 stirred up more popular resentment, and "business listened with a fascination that reduced it to palsied inertia." Business was simply unable to regain its feet, and nobody else seemed capable of providing the proper initiative or leadership. Even good intentions ended up damaging: publication of the names of banks to which the *Reconstruction Finance Corporation* had lent money aroused fears and doubts about the viability of those banks. This publicity was labeled a "most damnable and vicious thing" for it largely destroyed whatever benefits that agency might have brought.

In November 1932 the Governor

262 | *In his radio speech of March 12, the President outlined his plans for reopening the banks.*

ROOSEVELT APPEALS ON THE RADIO FOR FULL CONFIDENCE

of Nevada declared a statewide bank moratorium of twelve days in order to give them some respite. Many banks elsewhere closed in the face of runs. One consequence was an acute currency shortage. Companies and individuals had to issue scrip in order to pay salaries and meet other obligations. An incredible variety of these forms of emergency money was issued by almost four hundred communities throughout the states during 1932 and 1933. It ranged from pay warrants in anticipation of future taxes, to "prosperity checks" with space for 70 endorsements, to self-liquidating "stamp money." It was printed on wood, buckskin, and even seashells. Clearing House Certificates were printed in many cities during 1933. By then, however, the government had taken positive steps to assure sufficient currency.

On the Way to Recovery

The new year of 1933 brought only the foreboding of new trials and tribulations. On February 14th, the Governor of Michigan signed a proclamation closing all banks in his state for eight days. The money market reacted to this severe shock. Over 75 million dollars in currency was immediately withdrawn in Chicago alone. Fearful corporations tended to withdraw their funds from smaller banks to deposit them in New York or Chicago. Yet, even New York was not in a favorable position, for banks elsewhere that had deposited funds in New York were now removing them to meet their own obligations. "Bank deposits are money to be kept in circulation," the *Wall Street Journal* insisted in vain.

The drain on New York's gold supply also continued unabated. What was not earmarked for ship-

ment to London or Paris went into the satchels of hoarders. Long lines of frightened people formed in front of the Federal Reserve banks to exchange cash for gold. But, as the New York Clearing House Committee said on March 4th: "The unthinking attempt of the public to convert over 40 billion dollars of bank deposits into currency at one time is on its face impossible." That was the day Governor Herbert Lehman had to proclaim a two-day bank holiday. His proclamation was followed within hours by one from Governor Horner of Illinois. The same step was taken in numerous other states, while still others set a limitation on withdrawals. Panic and hysteria swept the country. The day that Franklin D. Roosevelt was inaugurated in Washington, the country at large was in complete financial chaos.

In his inaugural address, President Roosevelt tried to dispel

MANY BANKS IN THE CITY AND NATION REOPEN TODA

Keep your dollars _moving!_

PROSPERITY
STRAIGHT
AHEAD

SIGNS OF

Prominent Speakers · Fine Music
Saturdays . . . 7:15 P.M.
KFI—KGO
"BACK TO GOOD TIMES"

The nation's dollars are rapidly getting back to work. Confidence and common sense are with us again. [人]

ALL LOS ANGELES BANKS RENEW BUSINESS TODAY

End of Holiday Launches Upturn Over Nation, With Deposits Rising and Shoppers Crowding Stores

[BY THE ASSOCIATED PRESS]

From every part of the nation, the end of the bank holiday brought tangible signs of an upturn in business.

While banks reopened in the twelve Federal Reserve cities,

263 / *Confidence was the keynote of this* Bank of America *advertisement.*

132

"nameless, unreasoning, unjustified terror" and to instill new confidence and hope: "Our distress comes from no failure of substance. We are stricken by no plague of locusts . . . Plenty is at our doorstep, but a generous use of it languishes in the very sight of supply." A series of decisive actions followed in quick succession. On March 4th the President summoned Congress into extraordinary session, and also declared a four-day nationwide bank holiday "in order to prevent the export, hoarding or earmarking of gold and silver coin or bullion or currency." Although the closing of all banks imposed many hardships, these decisive measures were accepted with approval by the nation. Banks were authorized to set aside cash only for the most urgent payroll demands and to alleviate severe personal distress. Scrip became a necessity. It is said that in Pasadena, California, one

of the large hotels had to print scrip in a great hurry to help stranded millionaires. In New York the *American Bank Note Company* had to run night shifts to keep pace with demands. There was considerable opposition to scrip, plus a few positive ideas. The Mormons in Salt Lake City, for example, wanted to issue paper negotiable for services and merchandise, but worthless if deposited in a bank. Clearing House certificates were prepared in many parts of the country to wait for an official distribution order which never came.

Nine hours after convening, Congress passed the *Emergency Banking Relief Act* which the President signed into law on March 9, 1933. It granted extraordinary executive powers regarding currency, foreign exchange, and gold. The President immediately proclaimed an embargo on gold ex-

ports, while the Federal Reserve Board ordered gold hoarders to return their purchases not later than March 13th. Long lines soon were forming again in front of the Federal Reserve banks, but this time the gold—over 200 million dollars worth—changed hands in the other direction.

The Treasury and the Federal Reserve directed their efforts towards restoring normal banking operations. Roosevelt authorized the reopening of banks beginning March the 13th. However, their soundness had to be ascertained. First to reopen were banks operating under the Federal Reserve and Clearing House regulations; these were followed by all other banks which had been investigated and found sound. Hours before the first banks reopened the President addressed the nation over the radio. On Sunday evening, March the 12th, he paid tribute to the fortitude of a people that

264 | *An active recovery program began in early 1933.*

had accepted the hardships of the banking holiday. He stressed the role of banks in putting "money to work to keep the wheels of industry and agriculture turning around," and warned that "We do not want and will not have another epidemic of bank failures." He concluded on a strong note of hope: "Confidence and courage are the essentials of success in carrying out our plan. . . . You people must have faith; you must not be stampeded by rumors or guesses. Let us unite in banishing fear. We have provided the machinery to restore our national system; and it is up to you to support and make it work."

When the first banks to be certified under the *Emergency Banking Act* started opening, confidence had been restored. Deposits by far exceeded withdrawals. Beginning in 1934 the number of banks—which had declined steadily since 1918 and dropped catastrophically from 24,000 in 1930 to 14,800 in 1933—started slowly to increase.

Still, an unavoidable question suggested itself: how was it possible to have a breakdown of such dimensions? It could not be attributed to the inelasticity of the currency as in the 19th century, nor to a lack of adequate reserves —not in the richest country in the world. What was missing was a central power capable of maintaining coordination throughout the entire nation. Meeting this need was the purpose of the *Banking Act* of 1935, which shored up the power of the Federal Reserve Board.

In accordance with the President's command to "Put people to work" Congress began legislating recovery measures in 1933. It created numerous federal credit agencies to help farmers, small businessmen, and homeowners. By December 1940 there were 29 such agencies. Of paramount im-

portance was the *Federal Deposit Insurance Corporation*—the *FDIC*—established by Congress in 1933. By insuring accounts of member banks—initially up to $5,000, today up to $40,000—it acted as a psychological deterrent against panic. The FDIC also resulted in more stringent government supervision. In the words of a banking historian: "Since the government, by centralization of policy and detailed supervision of financial institutions, influenced the operations of an individual bank to a greater extent than ever before, it was logical that government should guarantee the assets of each bank, as far as the general public was concerned." Thus, out of one of the most tragic crises in the nation's financial history grew constructive and promising legislation.

133

265 / Check processor, 1973.

Banks and Their Role in Our Society

In contemporary society banks have acquired a new dimension bringing them closer to the everyday life of the average citizen. While continuing to provide the main source of financing for the nation's industry and commerce, as well as for the country's expansion into a worldwide financial involvement, banks have greatly increased their concern with the needs of the average man. Present-day banks have been compared to department stores of finance which fulfill a great variety of functions pertaining to individual pecuniary needs. This was not always the case. Only since the turn of the century and the establishment of the "Morris Plan" have small personal bank loans repayable in long-term installments become commonplace. Spurred by growth in consumer incomes and

demands, banks extended an increasing number of loans for the purchase of customers buying homes or automobiles. The scope of consumer demands for which loans are available has been expanding steadily in recent years. Yet, by no means does that make up the full picture of banking even today, for banks remain heavily involved in financing industry, business, and agriculture, as well as in handling the bonds which provide the mainstay of community improvements and development programs. Nevertheless, the emphasis on serving consumer demands has been responsible for a number of remarkable innovations such as banking by mail, drive-in banks, walk-up windows, and twenty-four-hour banking. These not only make banking more convenient but also stimulate business and especially streamline and even reduce the cost of banking operations.

135

You can bank all over the world and still be in North America.

Our International Banking Division is run with the skill, efficiency and personalized attention you've come to expect from North America. And we offer a world of banking services, including letters of credit, acceptance financing, purchase and sale of foreign exchange, and much more. So if you have business in a foreign country, be sure to come to North America first. We'll make you feel right at home. For more information, write: National Bank of North America, 44 Wall Street, New York, N.Y. 10005. Cable: INTIMATE. Tel: (212) 623-4000.

266 / The capitals of the world are within easy reach of many American banks.

VARIOUS FORMS OF CHECKS

267 | From hand-written check, to check encoded with magnetic ink.

268 | "Gold" check signed by President Ulysses S. Grant.

269 | Check imprinted in the center with a two-cent stamp for a tax imposed in 1862.

270 | Ration check.

271 | Template for check writing by blind people.

Important facets to the picture of today's banking system include branch banking and bank holding companies. Branching is something that began almost at the very beginning of banking in the United States. Later, some states completely prohibited branching, or else confined it within municipal or county boundaries. No branching beyond state lines is authorized even today. Branching is most common in the east and the west, while the central states have tended to favor the unit or single bank principle. Banking has also been directly affected by the rise of the bank holding company, or ownership by corporations. Total or partial ownership of banks by corporations has been closely regulated since 1956, when the *Bank Holding Company Act* prohibited companies from acquiring banks outside a single state. Still, interstate holding companies

272 / Chemically treated paper for checks.

anatomy of a check...

CHECK PROCESSING IS AUTOMATED. HIGH-SPEED ELECTRONIC MACHINES SORT CHECKS BY "READING" MAGNETIC INK CHARACTERS PRINTED ALONG THE BOTTOM OF CHECKS ... AT A SPEED OF ABOUT 60,000 CHECKS AN HOUR.

CHECK ROUTING SYMBOL: THE FIRST TWO DIGITS ARE BLANK BANK'S FEDERAL RESERVE DISTRICT NUMBER. THE THIRD DIGIT IS THE FEDERAL RESERVE OFFICE (HEAD OFFICE OR BRANCH) OR THE DESIGNATION OF A SPECIAL COLLECTION ARRANGEMENT. THE FOURTH DIGIT DESIGNATES BLANK BANK'S STATE OR A SPECIAL COLLECTION ARRANGEMENT.

BLANK BANK'S IDENTIFICATION NUMBER.

MR. FOWLER'S ACCOUNT NUMBER.

DOLLAR AMOUNT ... USUALLY ENCODED IN MAGNETIC INK CHARACTERS BY THE FIRST BANK TO RECEIVE THE CHECK.

BLANK BANK'S IDENTIFICATION NUMBER (NUMERATOR) OVER ITS CHECK ROUTING SYMBOL (DENOMINATOR). BOTH PARTS ARE ENCODED IN MAGNETIC INK ACROSS THE BOTTOM OF THE CHECK, EXCEPT THE FIRST TWO DIGITS OF THE NUMERATOR. THESE DIGITS ARE CITY, STATE OR OTHER TERRITORIAL DESIGNATIONS NEEDED FOR HAND PROCESSING BUT NOT FOR ELECTRONIC SORTING.

273 / Check protectograph of the 1920s.

formed prior to 1956 continue to operate.

One of the most spectacular aspects of contemporary American banking is the global dimensions of its activities. The drive to establish branches of American banks in foreign countries had only isolated antecedents prior to World War II. One was the Drexel & Morgan Bank, which had an overseas branch in London. For a long time London remained the only foreign city with American banks, though a few were organized in Argentina during World War I, and, later, in Havana, Rome, and Paris. Although Congress officially sanctioned foreign banking in 1919 by passing a bill introduced by Senator Walker Evans Edge, the *Edge Foreign Banking Act*, a vigorous expansion abroad began to take place only in the late 1940s. This expansion attained considerable dimensions in the 1960s. Today, there are more than 1,300 branches and offices of American banks scattered over large portions of the globe.

Banks Defend Their Security

Naturally, money and banks have always attracted lawbreakers, and the fight against crime constitutes one of the most fascinating, action-filled chapters in the annals of banking. A major bank robbery occurred as early as 1798, when the *Bank of Pennsylvania* was held up for the substantial sum of $116,000.

275 | *Early safe used in the* First Bank of Illinois, *Shawneetown, 1816.*

During the early 19th century thieves seem to have been less daring than today—or else bankers were just luckier. Or, perhaps, only stories with happy endings were transmitted to later generations. Such a story involved a teller in a New York bank who was able to thwart a robbery simply by hitting the would-be thief with a paperweight. Another time, in 1821, the watchman at a Philadelphia bank chased burglars away by waving a sword at them. Earlier, a criminal who had robbed that same bank of a sizable amount in uncut bills had been apprehended through a strange turn of events. After returning to his boarding house with his loot, the thief started to cut up the sheets of paper notes into bills, discarding the clippings in the fireplace. There, they were found the next day by a little girl, a relative of the landlady, who showed them to a neighbor—who happened to be the porter at the bank. He recognized the clippings immediately, and the thief was soon apprehended. Bank robberies always have fascinated the public and of course bankers have considered them worthy of special attention. The *Bankers' Almanac* for 1852 included on its calendar of "memorable events" a $40,000 robbery that had taken place twenty-five years earlier at the Bank of Virginia in Petersburg.

A bank cashier or treasurer in the early 19th century did not have a very relaxing job. We are told that the treasurer of the *Society for Savings* in Hartford "carried the bank money in his pocket by day, and put it under his pillow at night." More commonly, however, money was kept in strong boxes, usually iron chests. In addition to heavy padlocks, many strong boxes also had a secret lock in the lid, "a peculiarity of which was that when the key was withdrawn

276 | *Reinforced security. A strong box in an early Georgia bank was lowered overnight in a deep well within the vault room and then covered with a trap door secured with a padlock.*

277 | Old and new protection systems. A shotgun under the counter was ready to foil any robber. A similar gun is in the collections of the Smithsonian Institution.

278 | But a sophisticated vault door seemed a better protection.

for the night and a knobbed projection pushed over the opening, it was supposed that a burglar would be unable to find the keyhole."

Later, toward mid-century, "burglar-proof" safes came into use. In 1851, a bank in Middletown, Connecticut paid for a similar safe four hundred fifty dollars. Often such "safes" were not very safe—a banking historian describes a "gorgeously painted and decorated sheet iron safe in which the treasures of the bank were nightly stored . . . that wonderful box, which would offer no more resistance to the modern burglar, than if constructed of pine. The simple but unbounded confidence with which the banker in those primitive times nightly placed all his treasures in that safe, located in a cheap, pine shanty, and retired to his 'peaceful couch' was the very sublimity of faith. It needed only a visit to a neigh-

boring blacksmith shop for a cold chisel, or to a carpenter shop for even a hatchet, as the only tools necessary for the enterprising burglar . . . and all the coveted treasures were within his reach."

Usually, "burglar-proof" locks were not very effective, nor, even, were combination locks a good safeguard until time locks came into use in the 1870s. After that, burglars often had no alternative but to blast their way into a safe. The employment of case-hardened steel made it impossible to drill holes in safes. By the 1870s bank vaults, especially vault doors, could withstand very heavy attacks. Vault doors also became quite marvelous in a mechanical sense—by the turn of the century doors weighing up to thirty tons were so delicately suspended that they would move at the slightest touch. But even as vaults became tougher and more sophisticated, burglars became more adroit and

resourceful. For the exclusive use of members of the *American Bankers Association* the famous *Pinkerton Detective Agency* compiled files of pictures and descriptions of professional criminals. The Pinkerton lists suggest that banks suffered less from burglars and robbers than from forgers, swindlers, and embezzlers. At one point during the 19th century, forgery became so common that many bankers stopped honoring checks unless presented by people they knew personally.

After the Civil War, bank robbers became more violent and a sinister lore began to adhere to outlaws, especially in the west. The notorious James brothers, Jesse and Frank, the Dalton brothers and their gang, and the Butch Cassidy gang left a trail of blood across much of the country. Terror was their weapon. The James gang had its own style: while several members were taking care of the

REWARD

$15,000 REWARD
FRANK JAMES
DEAD or ALIVE
$25,000 REWARD FOR JESSE JAMES
$5000 Reward for any Known Member of the James Band
SIGNED
ST. LOUIS MIDLAND RAILROAD

279 / Jesse James was killed for a similar reward.

280 / Boisterously, the Jesse James gang entere Russellville, Kentucky, to rob the bank in 1868

bank, others staged a noisy general commotion, riding around town, shooting and yelling like savages in order to create a diversion. Just as they lived by violence, most of the James gang died by it—many of them were shot by enraged private citizens. Jesse James himself was killed by two members of his own gang who were after a $10,000 reward offered by the Governor of Missouri.

Each generation had its Jesse James, and gangsters like John Dillinger, Pretty Boy Floyd, Baby Face Nelson spread terror, apprehension, and sometimes even a perverse admiration—among their contemporaries. And despite such protective devices as electronic alarms and photoguard systems, bank robbers continue to defy both the law and the technical ingenuity of those who try to thwart their activities.

The Check and Its Evolution

For the average bank customer the entire banking process consists of standing at a teller's window and exchanging cash, checks, or deposit slips. He is only vaguely aware of the very exacting and tedious work going on in the back room. The heavy ledgers have been replaced today by sophisticated bookkeeping machines, but always there are enormous stacks of checks to be processed.

The check, basically a written order for a bookkeeping transfer of funds from one account to another, came into use in the United States almost simultaneously with the earliest banks. Starting as an entirely handwritten document, the check had an evolution that often reflected the evolution of banking itself. Under the influence of the lavish design of bank notes in the mid-1800s, checks began to take on a

more decorative appearance. Bu the business-like approach of ou electronic age brought the checl back to a simple, straightforwarc document, provided only with th essential data required for th long trip through its processin channels.

Over the years there have beer many interesting sorts of specia checks. For example, there was th "ration check," used during Worl War II to transfer "points" ir various goods from one account t another. Also for the blind ther are special checks with template which guide the hand in writing and also provide space for braill notes for the user's persona records.

Methods of cancelling check have changed considerably, from hand cancellation initially, t perforation with special mallets to machine cancellation. Becaus counterfeiting of checks was serious problem in the early day

Occupation . . . .
Criminal Occupation . . Stall for sneaks
Age, 45 . . . . Height, 5 feet 2 inches
Weight, 133 . . . . Build . . . .
Complexion . . . . Dark
Color of Hair . . Black, mixed with gray
Eyes . , ... Blue. Nose . . . .
Style of Beard . . . .
Color of Same . . . .
Date of Arrest . . . . Jan. 12, 1895
Where Arrested . . . .
Crime Charged . . . . Sneak robbery
Peculiarities of Build . . . .
Features, Scars, Marks, Baldness,
etc. Under lip puckered when talking. Faint scar from a burn inside right arm. Ears pierced. One left lower tooth gold. Is a confirmed opium fiend.

Criminal Occupation . . . . Forger
Age . . 60. Height . . . . . . 5 feet 10 inches
Weight, 175. Build . . . .
Complexion . . . .
Color of Hair . . . . Gray
Eyes, Light hazel. Nose . . . .
Style of Beard . . . . Full
Color of Same, Grayish, streaked with red
Date of Arrest 1889
Where Arrested . . . .
Crime Charged . . . . Forgery
Peculiarities of Build . . Cowlick on front of head.
Features, Scars, Marks, Baldness, etc. Man of great intelligence. Thoroughly versed in scientific matters. Fluent talker. Knows all about churches and religious matters. Heavy tobacco chewer.

282 / "Don't Make a Move," a painting by Victor Dubreuil, 1900.

of banking, bankers devoted much attention to its prevention. The elaborate design of many checks during the mid-1800s acted as one deterrent. To prevent the fraudulent alteration of checks, special safety paper, chemically treated to show any erasure, was highly publicized in the late 19th century. Another preventative, one still in use today, is to imprint or perforate checks with a figure showing their upper limit.

Many people are not aware of the long and complicated journey a check takes after it leaves their hand. Actually, in its circuit from drawer to payee and back, a check may take any one of several different routes. If both drawer and payee have accounts at the same bank, its route is short, since the check will be processed inside that bank. If the drawer and payee have accounts at different banks in the same locality, the check is processed by the bank of deposit,

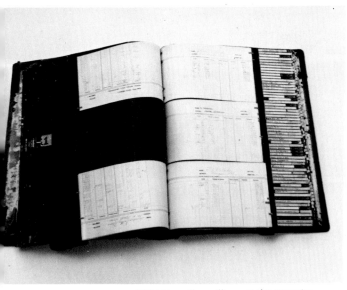

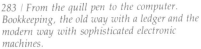

283 / *From the quill pen to the computer. Bookkeeping, the old way with a ledger and the modern way with sophisticated electronic machines.*

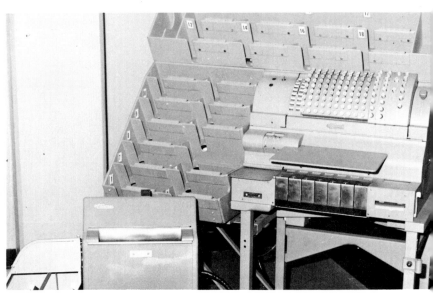

284 / *Postronic bookkeeping machine, 1959.*

142

then sent to the local clearing house, which processes it too and sends it along to the bank on which it was drawn; there, it is sorted, posted to the individual's account, microfilmed for a permanent record, returned to the file room to be cancelled, then cleared against the drawer's monthly statement. Only after all that is it returned to the drawer. If the two banks are in different localities and the check has to be sent to the District Federal Reserve Bank or a correspondent bank, its long circuit can include as many as fourteen steps or stations.

Banking in the Electronic Age

The processing of checks in a financially advanced country becomes an undertaking of gigantic proportions which entails enormous expenses. The great recent break-through came in 1959 from the *Bank Management Commission* of the *American Bankers Association.*

A special coding in magnetic ink was devised to guide checks through automated data processing machines. Through *Magnetic Ink Character Recognition,* or *MICR,* such vital information as the amount of the check, the identification of the bank, its Federal Reserve district, and the customer's account number, are transmitted and stored. In 1963, the American banking industry began coding checks with specially shaped Arabic numerals in a type called E-13B. Other countries, including Great Britain, Canada, and Japan, now use this code too. The characters used for *MICR* look like misshaped, broken-up numerals comprised of vertical and horizontal strokes of various thicknesses. Since they have to be readable not only to the human eye but also to the electronic decoder, they are printed on a band of specific width in magnetizable ink containing iron oxide.

285 / *Statement ledger machine, 1918.*

286 / Consumer transaction facility, 1970s.

These magnetic bands require a rigorously controlled printing, following exacting dimensional and qualitative specifications. When the encoded checks enter an automatic electronic computer reading and sorting equipment, the iron oxide particles become magnetized. They are scanned by a reading head which directs them to the proper compartment while the coded information is relayed to a data processor. Through the *MICR* program check processing has been infinitely speeded and the cost significantly reduced. Thus, technology has provided a solution to the problem of handling the astronomical quantity of checks produced every year—a temporary solution, at least.

The statistics regarding checks are awesome: in 1939 there were 27 million checking accounts in the United States and 3.5 billion checks written; in 1962 there were 58 million accounts and 14½ billion checks written for a total of 4.6 trillion dollars; in the next ten years these figures almost doubled, to 97 million accounts, 23 billion checks, and 10.6 trillion dollars. Since a seven percent annual increase seems to be the norm, it appears that even present-day processing equipment will shortly become inadequate. For a time the concept of a "cashless" or rather "checkless" society loomed at the horizon, and, while this does not seem to be an immediate possibility, it certainly has pointed in the right direction. A "less-check" operation seems to be the general goal. Even now, bank credit cards provide an instrument of payment which obviates the use of currency and helps reduce the number of checks. Pre-authorized payments, based on an authorization given to a bank by an account holder, also eliminate the use of checks. Moreover, bank customers in many places can have their banks take care of mortgage payments, utility bills, and paychecks without ever setting foot inside a bank's doors.

Some day, automation may entirely transform the banking system. With techniques for the electronic transfer of funds virtually perfected, and with the banking industry seriously considering such new means as voice print as an identification method for completing from the customer's home any type of banking transaction, anything seems possible in the future. Although it took almost 150 years to bring the banking concepts of Alexander Hamilton and Robert Morris to full fruition, it might take only decades for the electronic age to take complete hold of the American banking system.

Acknowledgements

The authors wish to thank the many individuals
and organizations for their help:

Mrs. Phyllis R. Abrams, *Assistant Curator, Girard College*—Dr. Rodney Armstrong, *Director, Boston Athenaeum*—Mr. Kenneth N. Bacon, *Vice President, The Bank of New York*—Mr. John U. Barton, *Manager, Special Activities, IBM, Armonk, N.Y.*—Mr. Q. David Bowers, *Los Angeles, California*—Mrs. Georgia B. Bumgardner, *Curator, Graphic Arts, American Antiquarian Society, Worcester, Massachusetts*—Mrs. Marjorie H. Burke, *Archivist, The First National Bank of Chicago*—*Chemical Bank, New York*—Mr. Samuel T. Clementis, *Akron, Ohio*—Mr. Paul G. Collins, *former Manager Public Affairs, Industrial National Bank, Providence, R.I.*—Mr. Benjamin M. Douglas, *Washington, D. C.*—Mrs. Merrilee Dowty, *Director, Wells Fargo Bank History Room, San Francisco*—*Federal Land Bank of Wichita, Kansas*—Mr. Leonard H. Finn, *West Roxbury, Massachusetts*—*First National Bank of Philadelphia*—*First Pennsylvania Bank, Philadelphia*—Mrs. Joan Gervino, Mrs. Ann Kessler, and Miss Susan Mester, *ABA Library, Washington, D. C.*—Miss Diane Henderson and Mr. C. J. Krause, *Frost National Bank, San Antonio, Texas*—Mr. Brent H. Hughes, *Falls Church, Virginia*—Mr. Earl Moore, *Wynnewood, Pennsylvania*—*Morgan Guaranty Trust Company of New York*—Mr. John A. Muscalus, *Bridgeport, Pennsylvania*—*National Bank of North America, New York*—Mr. Mortimer L. Neinken, *New York*—*New York Clearing House*—Mr. J. Roy Pennell, Jr., *Anderson, S.C.*—Mr. James F. Rogers, *Vice President, American Security and Trust Company, Washington, D. C.*—*Franklin D. Roosevelt Library, Hyde Park, N.Y.*—Mr. John L. Roper, II, *Norfolk, Virginia*—Mr. Robert R. Rosberg, *The Mosler Safe Company, Hamilton, Ohio*—Mrs. Margo Russell, *Coin World, Sidney, Ohio*—*The Second National Bank of Dayton, Ohio*—Mr. Neil Shafer, *Racine, Wisconsin*—Mr. Harvey G. Stack, *New York*.

Special thanks go to Mr. Albert R. Zipf, *Executive Vice President, Bank of America World Headquarters, San Francisco*, and to Mr. Jack Hull, *Manager, Mechanical Department, Bank of America, Dublin, California*, for the invaluable material provided.

The authors would like to express their appreciation for the assistance given by Dr. W. Liddon McPeters, *Chairman, American Bankers Association Centennial Committee*—Mr. Carl Levin, *Burson-Marsteller, Washington, D. C.*—Mr. Michael W. Delaney, *Public Relations, American Bankers Association*—Professor Oscar Tosi, *Michigan State University*—Mr. Robert B. Korver, Mr. Raymond J. Hebert, and Mr. Lynn W. Vosloh, *Division of Numismatics, National Museum of History and Technology*, and to Mr. Lucien R. Rossignol, *NMHT Library*, for their help in library research; also to Miss Carol Fifield and Mrs. Ellen Clain-Stefanelli, *Smithsonian Institution*, for the typing of the manuscript.

Picture Credits

National Museum of History and Technology, Smithsonian Institution, Washington, D. C.: Back cover, inside cover (lower half), 6, 7, 14, 32, 33, 34, 35, 40, 41, 43, 44, 46, 52, 53, 58, 60, 61, 65a, 65b, 67, 71, 74a-74f, 75, 76, 79, 80, 84, 86, 87, 88b, 88c, 92a-92q, 95b, 96b, 97a, 97b, 105, 106, 107, 114, 116b, 119b, 119c, 126, 127, 129a, 129c, 131, 132, 183a, 183b, 184, 207, 209b, 221, 223, 238, 239, 242, 259a, 259b, 260a, 260b, 267a-267d, 268, 269, 270, 272, 273, 283, 284, 285, color plates 1, 2, 3—*National Portrait Gallery, Smithsonian Institution, Washington, D. C.*: 39—*National Archives, Washington, D. C.*: 191, 234—*Library of Congress, Washington, D. C.*: 1, 3, 9, 50, 88a, 93a, 118, 139, 144, 145, 150, 151, 165, 175, 219, 220b, 230, 231, 232, 246, 247—*American Bankers Association, Washington, D. C.*: 47b, 226a, 226b, 267e, 281a, 281b—*American Antiquarian Society, Worcester, Mass.*: 13, 17, 19—*Bank of America, San Francisco*: 128a, 167—*The Bank of New York*: 20, 27—*Chemical Bank, New York*: 271—*Samuel T. Clementis, Akron, Ohio*: 30—*Milton S. Eisenhower Library, Johns Hopkins University, Baltimore*: 16—*Federal Land Bank of Wichita, Kansas*: 235—*The First National Bank of Philadelphia*: 193—*First Pennsylvania Bank, Philadelphia*: 23, 28, color plate 4—*Girard College, Philadelphia*: 73—*R. W. Glueckstein, Menominee Falls, Wis.*: 286b—*James M. Goode, Washington, D. C.*: 130—*International Business Machines Corporation, New York*: 265, 286—*Industrial National Bank, Providence, R.I.*: 45—*Liberty State Bank, Hamtramck, Mich.*: 129b—*Library Company of Philadelphia*: 25—*Morgan Guaranty Trust Company of New York*: Cover (lower half), Inside cover (upper half), 265a—*John A. Muscalus, Bridgeport, Pa.*: 74g—*Museum of the City of New York*: 110—*National Bank of North America, New York*: 266—*New York Clearing House*: 209a—*New York Historical Society*: 77—*Numismatic Antiquarian Society of Philadelphia*: 47—*J. R. Pennell, Anderson, S.C.*: 29, 189—*Pennsylvania Historical Society, Philadelphia*: 18—*Franklin D. Roosevelt Library and Museum, Hyde Park, N.Y.*: 264a—*John L. Roper, II, Norfolk, Va.*: 11, 12—*Swem Library, College of William and Mary, Williamsburg, Va.*: 4—*Wells Fargo History Room, San Francisco*: 117, 119a.

The following works have been particularly useful in obtaining pictures:

Album of American History, Vols. III-V, New York, 1946-60: 147, 152, 153, 218, 244, 245, 248—*The American Heritage History of the Thirteen Colonies*, New York, 1967: 15—*Bank Ad Views*, Wellesley Hills, Mass., 1975: 225—*Bankers' Almanac*, New York: 125, 186b, 197, 199—*Bankers' Magazine*, New York and Boston: 27, 122, 195, 196, 201, 204, 222, 224, 276, 277—*Banking*, New York: 206—Bathe, G., & D., Jacob Perkins, Philadelphia, 1943: 95a—Buel, J. W., *The Border Outlaws*, Chicago, 1880: 280—Cirker, H., & B., and the *Staff of Dover Publ.*, *Dictionary of American Portraits*, New York, 1967: 5, 22, 26, 56, 57, 69, 96a, 108, 112, 113, 120, 154, 156, 157, 158, 159, 161, 162, 163, 164, 166, 168, 169, 171, 173, 174, 233—Colt, C. C., & Keith, N. S. *28 Days*, New York, 1933: 252, 253, 257a, 261, 262—Cross, I., *History of Banking in California*, 4 vols., Chicago, 1927: 115, 116a, 227, 228—Crowell, M. A., *A Man who has Loaned Money to Millions*, *American Magazine*, March 1921: 237—Davis, A. M., *Colonial Currency Reprints*, Boston, 1910: 8—Dean, S., *History of Banking*, Boston, 1884: 36, 170—Diffenderffer, F. R., *History of the Farmers' Bank of Lancaster*, Lancaster, Pa., 1910: 62, 63, 64—*The Federal Reserve Bank*, New York, *The Story of Checks*, New York, 1972: 274—Gibbons, J. S., *The Banks of New York*, New York, 1858: 177, 178, 179, 180, 181, 182, 208a, 208b—Govan, T. R., *Nicholas Biddle*, Chicago, 1959: 82—Gras, N., *The Massachusetts First National Bank*, Cambridge, Mass., 1937: 31—Griffiths, W. H., *The Story of American Bank Note Company*, New York, 1959: 254—*Harper's Magazine*, New York: 93b-93d, 98a, 99a, 100a, 101, 102, 103, 104, 111, 124, 133, 134, 137, 138, 140, 142, 203, 205, 212, 213, 214, 215, 216—Herzog, P. W., *The Morris Plan*, Chicago, 1928: 238b—Hoggson, N. F., *Epochs in American Banking*, New York, 1929: 70—Holdsworth, J. T., *History of Banking in Pennsylvania*, 4 Vols., Chicago, 1928: 42, 54, 68—Huston, F. M., *History of Banking in Illinois*, Chicago, 1926: 275—James, F. C., *The Growth of Chicago Banks*, Chicago, 1938: 251—James, M., & B. R., *The Story of the Bank of America*, New York, 1954: 128b, 263—Johnson, W., *A Century of the National Bank of Germantown*, Philadelphia, 1914: 278—*King's Views of the New York Stock Exchange*, New York, 1898: 135, 136, 160—Lanier, H. W., *A Century of Banking in New York*, 1922: 66, 141, 176—*Frank Leslie's Illustrated*, New York: 91, 146, 188, 206, 210, 211, 217—Lewis, L., Jr., *History of the Bank of North America*, Philadelphia, 1882: 24, 51—Longacre, J., & Herring, J., *National Portrait Gallery*, 4 Vols., Philadelphia, 1836: 21, 49, 83, 85, 89—*Los Angeles Times*: 256, 257b, 257c, 262b—Low, L., *Hard Times Tokens*, Boston, 1886: 88d-88h, 90—*Minnesota Tribune*: 258—Mittler, M., *Eroberung eines Kontinents*, Zurich, 1968: 123a, 143, 148, 279—Nevins, A., *History of the Bank of New York*, New York, 1934: 38, 48, 202—Newman, E., *The Early Paper Money of America*, Racine, Wis., 1967: 10—*New York Times*: 220a, 246b, 255—Oberholtzer, E. P., *Jay Cooke*, Philadelphia, 1907: 185a, 185b, 186, 187—*Ormsby's Bank Note Engraving*, New York, 1852: 98b, 99b, 100b—*The Pageant of America*, Vol. IV & V, New Haven, Conn., 1927: 2, 59, 78, 81, 200, 236, 243, 244—Robertson, R., *The Comptroller*, Washington, D. C., 1968: 190, 192, 194, 250—*San Francisco Daily Herald*: 119b, 123b—St. Clair, L., *The Story of the Liberty Loans*, Washington, D. C., 1919: 240, 241—*United States Government Printing Office, Seals*, Washington, D. C. 1958: 229, 249a-249c, 264b-264h—Wainwright, N. B., *History of the Philadelphia National Bank*, Philadelphia, 1953: Cover (upper half) 55, 72—Williams, H. W., *Mirror to the American Past*, New York, 1974: 149, 282—Wilson, N., *400 California Street*, San Francisco, 1964: 121, 172, 198.